POGONIP

JEWEL OF SANTA CRUZ

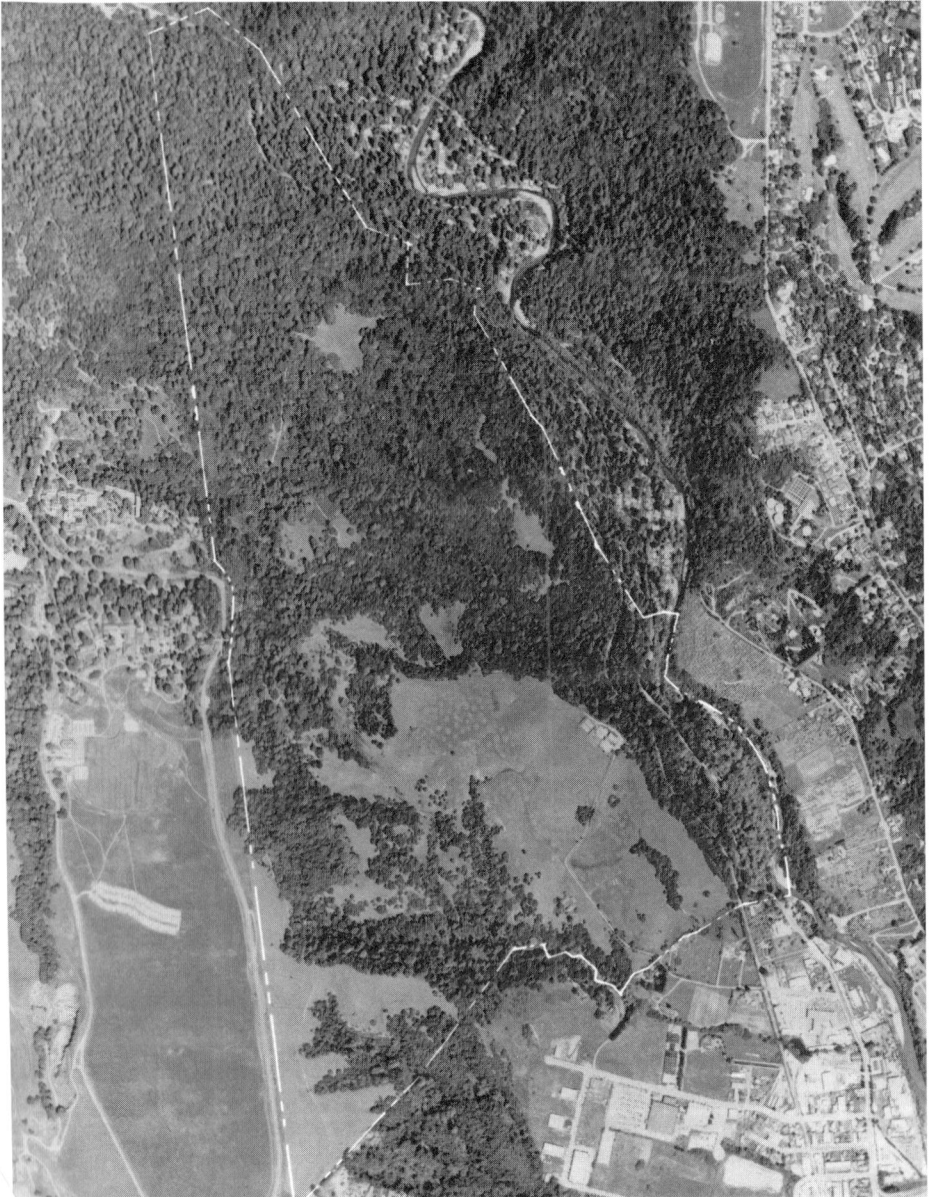

iew of Pogonip from the air before 1997, when Wavecrest was added; boundaries of
onip are shown by dotted white line; Harvey West in lower right corner; club-
at edge of central meadow. (courtesy of Rich Beale)

POGONIP

JEWEL OF SANTA CRUZ

Joan Gilbert Martin
&
Colleen McInerney-Meagher

To Mary & Roger
my dear friends.
We miss you in
the neighborhood!

Otter B Books

Love,
Colleen

Pogonip
Jewel of Santa Cruz

By Joan Gilbert Martin
&
Colleen McInerney-Meagher

Manufactured in the United States of America

Published by Otter B Books, Santa Cruz, California. Publisher and distributor of history and related topics of the Monterey Bay Area.

Series: Topics in Monterey Bay Area History

ISBN 978-1-890625-08-5

Main cover photo by James M. Morley. Back cover inset photos occur in the text where they are credited.

Contents

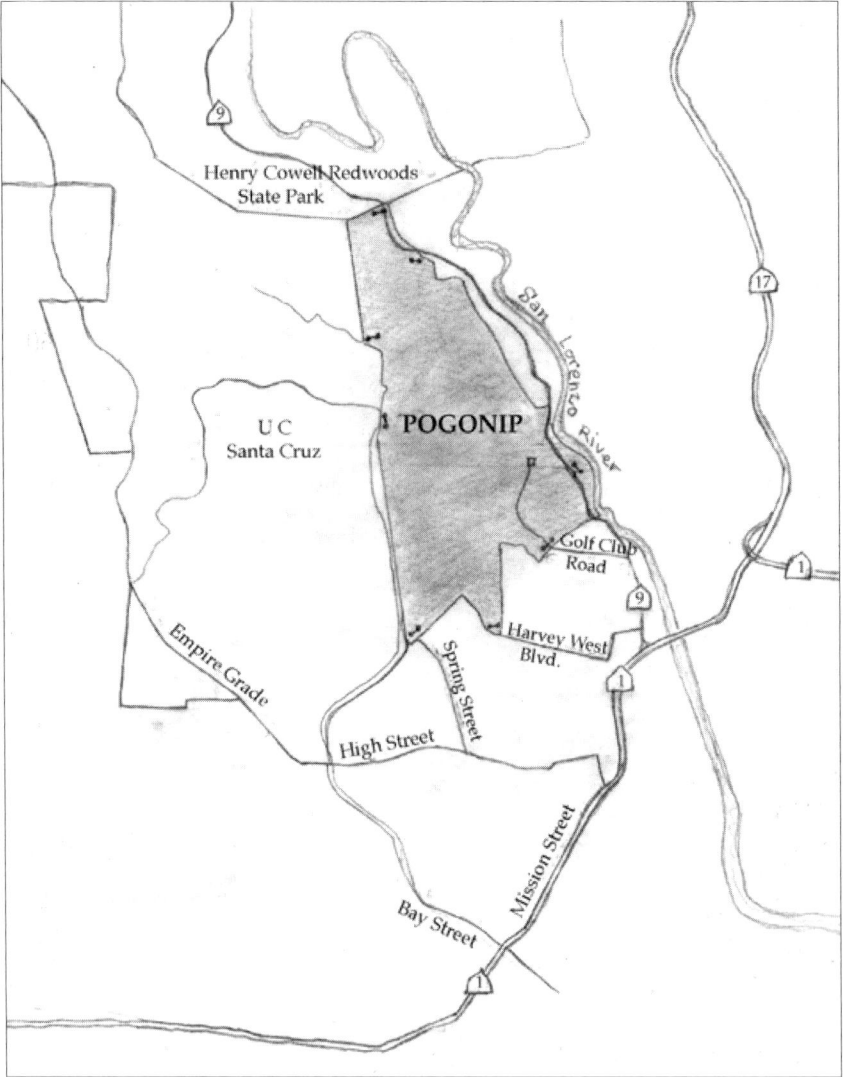

Henry Cowell Redwoods
State Park

San Lorenzo River

17

U C
Santa Cruz

POGONIP

Golf Club
Road

9

1

Empire Grade

Harvey West
Blvd.

Spring Street

1

High Street

Mission Street

Bay Street

1

Introduction

What is Pogonip?

Pogonip is an expanse of 640 scenic acres containing open meadows, woodlands, and streams. It belongs to the City of Santa Cruz and is managed by the city's Parks and Recreation Department. The entire expanse of Pogonip lies within the city limits just north of developed portions of Santa Cruz. Henry Cowell Redwoods State Park lies to the north, the University of California at Santa Cruz to the west, and unincorporated portions of Santa Cruz County to the east.

Pogonip truly is the jewel in the crown of the City of Santa Cruz. Within minutes of the center of a bustling city, Pogonip provides an oasis where peaceful contemplation of nature is possible.

Pogonip is more than just a place. This web of forest, meadows,

Pogonip prairie, forest and meadow, with a view looking south past the City of Santa Cruz to Monterey Bay. (Don Nielsen)

trails, and creeks is small, yet it evokes large hopes and visions. Some hopes have been realized, as this unique area is preserved from development. Other hopes are yet to be fulfilled: a garden where the homeless can grow food and flowers and their own self worth, and restoration of the historic clubhouse so it can once again grace the main meadow with its views of the city and the bay.

The visions are varied and imaginative. One vision sees Pogonip, with its gently rounded main meadow surrounded by forest, its fern-banked springs and streams, its small hidden meadows amid tall redwoods, as female in nature. Another vision imagines the main meadow as a ceremonial center where native people once joined together for spiritual communication, perhaps to dance and sing and tell stories. There are other visions, probably as many as there are visitors.

What we know to be true is that Pogonip was once an area where bear and antelope roamed in search of food and where the local native people, the Ohlone, gathered berries and acorns and hunted the bear and antelope. During the Mexican Era, it was part of the five-thousand-acre Rancho La Cañada del Rincón, named for the deep curve (rincón) in the San Lorenzo River that lies just north of today's Pogonip boundaries. In the last half of the nineteenth century, when lime and lumber dominated the Santa Cruz economy, Pogonip played a small but significant role. The Pogonip lime kilns were perhaps the first in the county; its limerock quarries and its extensive redwood forests supplied raw materials; and its roads were used to transport both lumber and lime.

In the twentieth century, Pogonip became a playground for Santa Cruz society. The first 18-hole golf course in the county was developed at Pogonip. When the golf course failed, the Pogonip Polo Club took over. Dedicated to women's polo, the club was a founding member of the United States Women's Polo Association. Women (and men) played polo there until after World War II. The Pogonip club continued through the years as a popular country club that catered to a family clientele. At the same time, an auto camp popular with out-of-town visitors thrived in the flats of Sycamore Grove along the San Lorenzo River.

The following chapters expand on this history to tell how Pogonip became a recreational area owned by the City of Santa Cruz, with natural resources available for the enjoyment of everyone.

The Name

Where did the name Pogonip come from and what does it mean? Fred Swanton, an early developer of the golf course on the Pogonip property, was quoted as saying that Pogonip means "a spot where the sun shines first." Dorothy Deming Wheeler, the founder of the Pogonip Polo Club, liked to say that Pogonip was *po* for polo, *go* for golf, and *nip* for that little nip at the bar. This was an apt name for the very social Pogonip Polo Club. However, neither Dorothy Wheeler nor Fred Swanton had it quite right. And, how Pogonip first came by its name remains a mystery.

What we do know is that Pogonip is an English word of Shoshone Paiute origin. It is used to "designate a peculiar fog that occasionally visits mountain country in the winter. The sun is obscured ... sometimes for days while the air is charged with a heavy fog in which fine particles of snow seem to be flying. Although the temperature may not be low, intense cold is felt because of the humidity that prevails." The Random House dictionary claims that the Shoshone word means "white death."[1]

An 1888 account of this fog from the journals of Alfred Doten of Virginia City, Nevada, describes it as follows: "'Pogonip hazed the air most of the day ... air full of fine floating sleety frost particles, glinting in the sun-light and collecting on tree twigs, bushes, horse hair and human beard – coldest fog in the world, and not often found on the Comstock."[2]

Several (probably unreliable) sources claim a tribe called Pogonip lived in the Santa Cruz area. Robert E. Burton, a Santa Cruz city councilman, county supervisor, and high school science teacher was one of those. He wrote in 1938, "[Pogonip] is indeed the name of a tribe of Indians, the first possessors of this delightful spot, who dwelt there long before the advent of the white man.... Some claim it to mean 'where the early morning rays strike first' (which is true), then others say it means 'frozen mist' which is also true of the lowlands beneath. Two very different meanings to be sure."[3] Tom McHugh in

1

Pogonip Fog, composed of tiny particles of ice, hovers low above the ground in front of Yosemite Falls.
(www.goldengate photo.com web site, #A05-2-9)

1959 also reports a Pogonip tribe here. He claims Pogonip Creek was "so called from the tribe of Indians that lived along its banks even to 45 or so years ago."[4] On the other hand, Donald Thomas Clark finds no evidence that a tribe of that name ever existed in this part of the county and is mystified how a Shoshone Paiute word was applied here.[5]

All dictionaries agree it is a Shoshone/Paiute word meaning icy or frozen fog; what no one understands is how it came to be applied to an area in Santa Cruz county that is not home to the Shoshone and does not suffer from pogonip fogs. There is no name for such a fog in the Awáswas language spoken by the local Ohlone tribelet, the Uypi. The Awáswas words for fog are either *sitis* or *metsheknes*, depending on the linguist; and the word for ice is *wákkan*.[6]

The Shoshone-speaking Paiute were distant neighbors to the south and southeast where true pogonip fogs were common. Possibly their word for fog percolated into local lore back in the mid 1800s during the time that the mission was closing and Native tribes were intermingling. Another possibility is that, in the 1850s, Truckee Indians from Nevada brought the name with them when they spent winters in Santa Cruz. Or perhaps it was American visitors from Nevada and eastern California who brought the name to this area.

Encountering the low ground fogs near the rivers and streams of the Pogonip property, these early visitors might have named the area for the icy fogs they knew back home.[7] It is also possible that the local fogs might have been icier in those days, as the so-called "Little Ice Age" had not yet ended.

Nevertheless, the name is definitely one that appears in Santa Cruz as the name of a creek, a volunteer fire company, and that area of the county we now call Pogonip. The name was mentioned here as early as 1875 when it was given to the Pogonip Rifle Team that competed in the area.[8] Local tanner, Henry Kron, was a member of this club. Kron also gave the name to the Pogonip Hose Company formed November 1, 1885, by employees of his tannery.

The early 1880s had seen a number of these hose companies that fought local fires: The Alerts and Pilots with cart houses on Pacific avenue; the Relief company on Mission Hill; and the Kirby company to protect the Kirby tannery on upper Laurel street. The Pogonip cart house was located on River Street across the street from the Kron tannery and adjacent to Golf Club Drive, which later led up to

Pogonip #3 Hose Cart House still standing in 1952 on River Street at the foot of the road leading up to the Pogonip property.
(Dorothy Deming Wheeler Scrapbooks)

the Pogonip Polo Club. The Pogonip Fire Cart itself was bright red with nickel trim and had been the gift of H. F. Kron, owner of the tannery.[9] The cart is still preserved at Fire Station No. 3 on Younglove and Mission streets in Santa Cruz.

Pogonip Creek was perhaps named for the fogs that can still be found in its vicinity. The creek is a small intermittent stream that flows down from Pogonip into the area between Golf Club Road and Pioneer Street. It broadens out into to a small pond, called Salz Pond, on what was Kulman & Salz Tanning Company land.[10] From there it flowed openly to the San Lorenzo River. Today, its terminus is buried under the concrete of an industrial area.

Robert E. Burton described Pogonip Creek in 1938 as follows: "Near the northern boundary of Santa Cruz city, but still within its limits, the Big Tree road[11] crosses a small stream called Pogonip .... The headwaters of that stream are about one mile west and halfway up the hill, in one of the most secluded and pleasant spots of Santa Cruz. Arriving at the headwaters of that stream, you find a live spring, gushing forth from the mountainside and from beneath the roots of magnificent redwood and bay trees. Typical of many springs of the limestone regions, it gushes forth with full force, giving rise to an entire stream, which cascades on its way eastward."[12]

Drawing of the headwaters of Pogonip Creek, looking east over the polo fields of the Pogonip Polo Club.
(Robert E. Burton, October 1938)

4

Chapter One

Native Peoples

The Ohlone

Before "first contact" with the Spaniards, the native peoples of the California coast had a hunting-gathering way of life. As these people kept no written records, we have only a general picture of their life from reports in the diaries of European settlers, and observers. The Spanish mission baptismal records name the villages the native converts came from, thus providing a more detailed count of village populations. The Ohlone, a collective name given to the people of the Central California Coast, populated an area between San Francisco and Big Sur.

These people were organized into small groups or tribelets living in one, two, or three semi-permanent villages, each village with 50 to 150 persons. In addition to their villages, each group claimed various campsites to which they moved seasonally for the purpose of fishing or hunting or for gathering seeds, berries, and acorns. The entire coastal area was sparsely settled—anthropologists estimate there were perhaps as few as two to four people per square mile.[1] Anthropologist A. L. Kroeber estimated the entire Ohlone population at around 7,000 people.[2]

The villages shrank and grew depending on the season. In the winter they lived near the water where they fished and collected shellfish. The men hunted deer throughout the year and wild fowl in the spring and fall. In the spring and early summer, the women traveled inland to the meadows where they collected seeds. As the summer waned, the entire village traveled to the inland hills where the oak trees provided their staff of life, the acorn.[3]

Throughout the coastal area, live oaks thrived as well as small stands of black oak. In the Santa Cruz Mountains, including the

Pogonip area, were large stands of tanoaks, a favorite source of acorns. The Pogonip area provided seed meadows and berry patches, as well as oak groves. Each small group claimed its own meadow or acorn patch. No archeological evidence currently exists of permanent sites at Pogonip. The nearest permanent sites for which there is evidence are found in the developed areas just to the south of Pogonip.[4]

Local Tribelets

The records kept at Mission Santa Cruz name the tribelets living in the Santa Cruz area, giving each its saint's name as well as its native name. Of these, the Uypi (or San Daniel) is the group that populated the mouth of the San Lorenzo River and what is now the City of Santa Cruz. These were the people who gathered seeds, berries, and acorns, and hunted on the land we call Pogonip. No tribelet named Pogonip lived in the area.

Neighboring groups of the Uypi include the Cotoni or Santiago to the northwest (near Davenport), the Aptos or San Lucas to the east, the Sayante or San Juan to the northeast (Zayante Creek and Scotts Valley).[5] Each Ohlone tribelet spoke a different dialect, all part of the larger

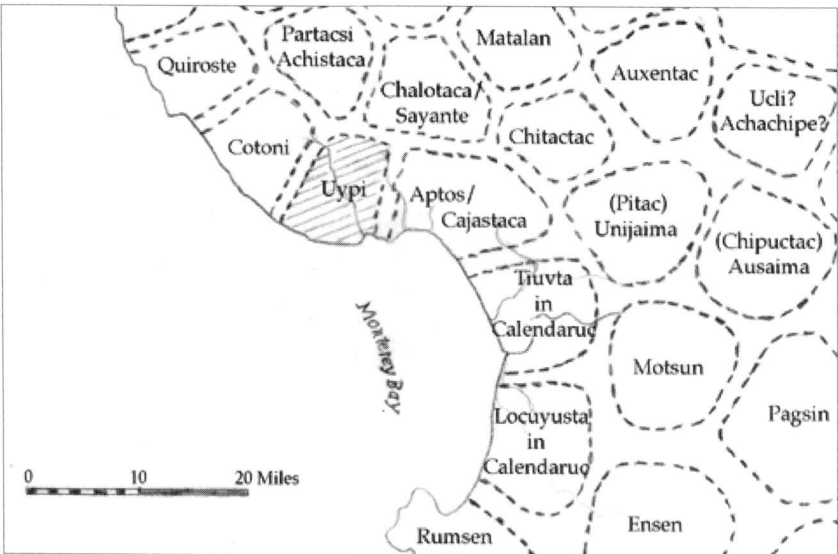

The general locations of tribelets in the Monterey Bay Area. (Adapted from map by Western Anthropological Research Group, Inc.)

6

Penutian language family. The Esselen people to the south spoke a completely unrelated language, part of the Hokan language family. To the east and southeast, people such as the Paiute and Mono, spoke languages in another distinct language family, the Shoshone.[6]

First Contact

Imagine the consternation of these people when Spaniards wearing armor and riding horses and mules appeared in their land. The Ohlone had lived a settled and unchanging life here for many hundreds of years before the arrival of the Europeans. During this extended period of time they had achieved something quite rare in human history: a way of life that gave them relative peace and stability.

Now, into this ancient way of life appeared the Spaniards. They proceeded to build a series of missions to which, with the best of

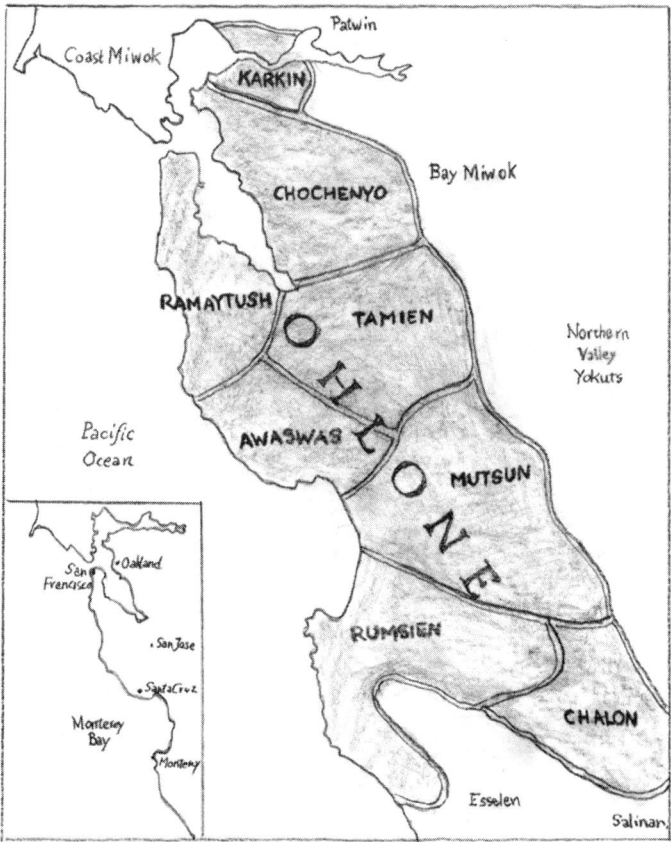

Map showing where the eight Ohlone language groups were spoken. (*A Gathering of Voices*, Museum of Art & History)

intentions, they lured the local Indians to be baptized. When Mission Santa Cruz was founded in 1791, many members of local tribal groups, including the Uypi, moved into this Mission.

It is not clear exactly why the Indian peoples moved so willingly to the missions. Perhaps they came because of their interest in the new and exciting technologies brought by the Spaniards, who had looms, mirrors, beads, metal pots, iron tools, and guns; and who had new and interesting foods, such as sugar and cocoa. Perhaps at first the Mission offered protection. But later, as the populations were decimated by disease, the tribal groups had insufficient people to survive on their own. Then, perhaps, some Indian people moved to the Missions as a last resort.[7]

The Uypi people were the first group to be completely absorbed by Mission Santa Cruz. The last group to be absorbed were Yokuts speakers from the San Joaquin Valley, who were brought there after 1808. During the course of the Mission period, the distinct Indian language barriers broke down and tribal groups essentially lost their identities. Because of the high death rates, intermarriage between speakers of distinct languages took place: many Ohlone-speakers married Yokuts-speakers from the east and Esselen-speakers from the Big Sur area to the south, resulting in an intermingling of languages. Such intermarriages would never have occurred in pre-mission times.

When the Mexican government secularized the missions in 1834, the Indian inhabitants were turned out to fend for themselves. Some of the Yokuts newcomers returned to their old homelands in the central valley, but the local Ohlone and other newcomers stayed on to work on the ranchos and homes owned by descendants of the Spanish invaders of sixty years earlier.[8] After the mission era, the Indian groups that had lived here successfully for hundreds of years were absorbed into the labor force on the ranchos, often taking Hispanic names. Though it might seem as if they disappeared, they did not; they are still here.

Chapter Two

The Early Years

The Mexican Era

The first Europeans to settle in the Santa Cruz area were the Spaniards. They founded the Santa Cruz, "Holy Cross," Mission in 1791 more than twenty years after the establishment of the Presidio at Monterey in 1770. Santa Cruz was not on El Camino Real, the King's Highway, which connected many of the Spanish missions. Guarded by swamps along Monterey Bay and with a rugged mountainous coastline to the north, the native people of Santa Cruz remained isolated long after members of neighboring tribes had joined missions.

In 1797, in order to secure their possession of California, Spain established the third secular town of Alta California, the Villa de Branciforte. Built on the plateau across the San Lorenzo River from the mission, the few townspeople who arrived from Mexico struggled to survive insufficient Spanish support and continual bickering with the mission priests.

Mexico won its independence from Spain in 1822 and took over the governance of California. Although Spain had governed this, its most distant territory, with a light hand, under Mexico the territory suffered full-scale neglect. The Mexican governors were, however, generous in dispensing land grants and the *Californios*, as the Hispanic people living in Alta California were called, raised cattle on huge ranchos. They developed a pastoral life style that was largely self-sufficient—raising most of what they needed on their ranchos—though they traded with the rare ship that called along the coast, and dried cowhide became known as the "California dollar."

Because this Pacific edge of our continent was totally isolated from the industrious Atlantic seaboard, the *Californios* might have continued their pastoral existence for many years had it not been for the discovery of gold in California in January of 1848 and the resulting influx of American and European settlers.

The American Era

On February 2, 1848, coincidentally just nine days after gold was discovered on the American River, the Treaty of Guadalupe-Hidalgo ended the brief Mexican War and gave control over Alta California to the American military, beginning what is called the American era.

Thus, when the rush for gold brought the huge influx of Americans into the state, they already had a government that would support them in their desire for land. By September of 1850, California was a state within the United States of America. Within a few years, a large number of people poured into California. It has been estimated that more than 300,000 people arrived in California between the years 1848 and 1854[1] Many came and left within a relatively short time; others stayed longer; and still others remained permanently.

Rancho La Cañada del Rincón

The land that later became Pogonip was originally part of the Rancho La Cañada del Rincón en el Rio San Lorenzo de Santa Cruz, that is, the "Ranch of the Valley of the Curve in the San Lorenzo River of Santa Cruz" or, less formally, Rancho La Cañada del Rincón. The rancho was given that name because it included a deep horseshoe curve of the San Lorenzo River, known as El Rincón or "the corner."[2] This curve in the river is found in what is now Henry Cowell Redwoods State Park, just north of Pogonip.

Rancho La Cañada del Rincón was granted in 1843 as two square leagues to Pierre Sansevain, a Frenchman. After statehood, the rancho was confirmed in 1855 to "Don Pedro Sansevaine" (as he was then called) and in 1858 it was patented as 5,827 acres bordered by the Ranchos Zayante, San Augustin, La Carbonera, Refugio, and by the lands of the Santa Cruz Mission.

Pierre Sainsevain came to the United States from the Bordeaux region of France in 1837. He first worked for his uncle Jean Louis Vignes at his vineyard in Los Angeles. Vignes, who had arrived in California in 1831, was an important figure in early California viticulture. He imported European cuttings and offered his first

Boundaries of the Ranchos called Refugio, Cañada del Rincón, La Carbonera, Zayante, and San Augustin, and the relation of these ranchos to the City of Santa Cruz in the 1890s. (Adapted from 1902 *Santa Cruz Quadrangle* map, Earth Sciences & Map Library, UC Berkeley)

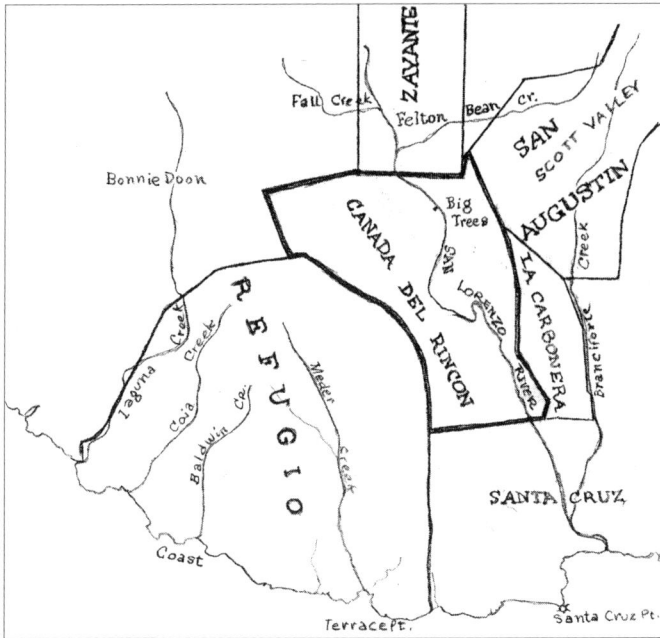

vintage in 1837. In 1850, Pierre Sainsevain brought Vignes' wines and brandies by ship to Monterey. This was the first known shipment of California wines over a considerable distance.[3]

Sainsevain was a man of many interests and of considerable prominence in early California. By 1841 he had moved to northern California and was living in San Jose. In 1845, two years after being granted the Rancho La Cañada del Rincon, he married Paula Suñol, the daughter of Don Antonio Suñol.[4] From 1846, Sainsevain was in partnership with Charles Roussillon, a fellow Frenchman. Together, in January of 1846, they launched the schooner *Santa Cruz*, which Roussillon had built for Sainsevain.[5]

According to the alcalde records of 1846, Sainsevain was granted the right to build a sawmill in Santa Cruz on April 25 of that year.[6] He built the mill on the flat below the curve in the San Lorenzo River, commonly called El Rincón. This area was subsequently known as Powder Mill Flat because the powder works were later located there. He ran the mill with his partner Charles Roussillon and, later, with Samuel J. Hensley.[7] Sainsevain went to the mines in 1848. In 1849 he was back in Monterey as a representative from San Jose at the Constitutional Convention. He became one of the 48 signatories to

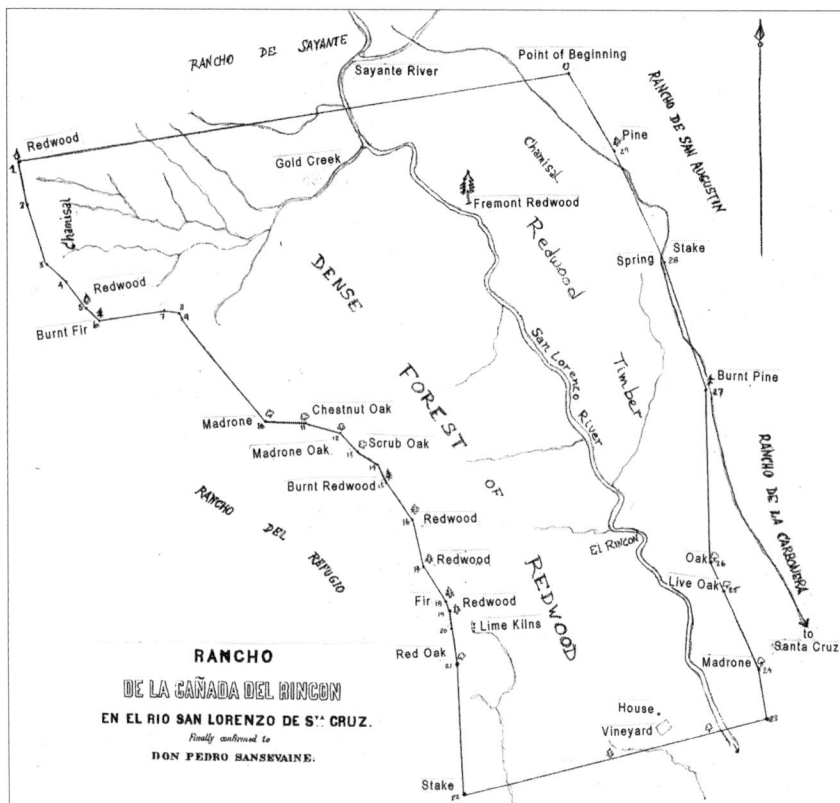

Adapted from an 1855 map by the U.S. Surveyor General's Office that shows La Cañada del Rincón rancho. Notice the surveyors markers are frequently trees, sometimes burnt trees. The portion of the rancho that became Pogonip is in the lower right, below el Rincon and just west of the San Lorenzo River. (Special Collections, University Library, UC Santa Cruz)

the new constitution of the State of California. In 1859, Sainsevain and his partners sold their interest in Rancho La Cañada del Rincón to Albion P. Jordan and Isaac E. Davis. After selling the rancho, Sainsevain concentrated on wine making. He died in Bordeaux, France in October 1904.[8]

Jordan & Davis

Albion P. Jordan and Isaac E. Davis were two young engineers from the East who had arrived in San Francisco by 1850. They reportedly met while working for a delta steamship that ran between

12

San Francisco and Sacramento. Learning that the local limerock was of good quality, they quit the steamship company and went into the lime business. According to one source, Jordan knew about limerock and lime because his father had been a lime manufacturer in Maine.[9]

The two men moved to Santa Cruz in 1853 and built their first Santa Cruz kilns that same year, at what is now the corner of Bay and High streets.[10] Later, in 1859, they bought the Rancho La Cañada del Rincón from Pierre Sainsevain and his partners. On their new rancho they quarried limerock, harvested cordwood, and successfully produced lime. They also built a wharf and owned ships with which to transport the lime. By then, they were the largest lime manufacturers in the state.[11]

Two large lime kilns, probably built in the 1850s, sit far above the old Rincon Road in that part of Rancho Rincon that became Pogonip. The south kiln has three doorways, the north kiln four. The kilns are set into the hillside to support the back wall. Almost directly behind and above the kilns is a large limerock quarry. It is

Team of oxen hauling cordwood on the Rincon Road through Pogonip. (Photo by Lillian Howard, Geoffrey Dunn collection)

The Lime Industry

Santa Cruz was a major center of the lime industry for many years, primarily because it had large deposits of limerock, the raw material used to make lime. Lime, produced in small quantities, was first used here to build the Santa Cruz Mission. Later, after statehood, lime became the second largest industry, after timber, in Santa Cruz. Santa Cruz's location on Monterey Bay enabled easy transport of the lime by boat to San Francisco, the primary market. Today, lime has a myriad of uses in many industries, but in the nineteenth and early twentieth century it was used primarily for construction. It was the principal ingredient in mortar, plaster, and stucco.

Santa Cruz not only had an abundance of limerock, but also a plentiful supply of timber. Limerock was converted to lime by heating it in kilns at temperatures of 2,000 degrees F. over several days. These high temperatures were maintained by burning wood, mostly the local redwood. Some estimates say it took 70 cords of wood to complete a single burn. Of course that number depended on the size of the kiln. In any case, the kilns required immense quantities of wood. The local industry used 3,000 cords in 1860, 10,000 cords in 1880, and 14,000 cords in 1884.[12] As a result, the lime companies needed to own timberland as well as limerock quarries.

North lime kiln at Pogonip, taken in 1900. Notice the growth of trees, indicating that these kilns were not in use at that time and had probably not been used for many years. (Museum of Art & History @ the McPherson Center)

uncertain who built these lime kilns or when they were built. What is known is that, in 1859, James Frazier Reed and his son-in-law, Frank Lewis, were using the facility. Reed and Lewis were still burning lime there when Jordan and Davis acquired Rancho Rincón in late 1859.[13] It is unlikely that Davis and Jordan, or later, Davis & Cowell burned lime in the Pogonip kilns.

In 1862, Davis and Jordan set up a sawmill on the Rincon ranch.[14] It was "situated about a mile and a half beyond Reed's old lime kiln, and about four miles from the beach," about where Rincon station was later established.[15] By 1866, Davis and Cowell had built a road—from its description the Rincon Road—that was probably used to haul lumber from the Rincon mill down to Bay Street and thence to the company wharf.[16]

In 1875 the Santa Cruz & Felton railroad opened a station at Rincon.[17] At this time, Rincon Road would have been used to haul cordwood from Rincon Station to the Bay Street kilns. By 1885, Davis and Cowell were shipping lime by railroad from their Rincon warehouse. The lime probably was taken along Rincon Road to the railroad and the road would also have been used haul empty lime barrels back to the kilns.[18] At one point, in 1887, Davis and Cowell proposed a branch line to the railroad that would run along the route of the Rincon Road.[19] This line was never built, and Rincon Road continued to be used to haul lime, empty lime barrels, and cordwood well into the 1900s. The macadamized remains of Rincon Road still run north/south through Pogonip as the Rincon and Spring Trails.

In the early 1860s, Jordan's health began to fail, and in 1865 he sold his interest in the firm of Davis and Jordan to Henry Cowell. Jordan returned to his home in Maine where he died in November of 1866, but not before building one last ship, the *A. P. Jordan*. His family brought his remains back to Santa Cruz, where he was buried.[20]

The Cowell Family

Henry Cowell and his family are important to the history of Pogonip. The Cowell family and later the S. H. Cowell Foundation were owners of the land that became Pogonip for well over a hundred years. They acquired the land in 1865 and kept it until 1989 when the foundation sold the land to the City of Santa Cruz.

Henry Cowell arrived in California with his brother John before 1850; certainly they were in business in San Francisco by that date.

Entrance to the residence on the Cowell Home Ranch. The ranch house, now called Cardiff House after long-time ranch manager George Cardiff, still stands on what is now UCSC property. The house has been provost lodging and is now the University Women's Center. (*Overland Monthly*, July 1912)

Their business was probably drayage and storage. In 1853, their assets included a warehouse and a wharf. By 1865, Henry had taken control of the business from his brother.

In 1865, Henry Cowell bought Jordan's share of the firm of Davis and Jordan. The sale included the Rancho Cañada del Rincón, except for the site of the Powder Works, which Davis and Jordan had previously sold.[21] Henry Cowell then moved to Santa Cruz where he lived with his family on the ranch where the lime operation had long thrived. The company was now known as the firm of Davis and Cowell.[22]

The Cowells eventually owned many ranches in California, but the ranch in Santa Cruz was always their favorite. Known as the Cowell Home Ranch, the family lived there from 1865 until 1879 and visited frequently thereafter, returning in the summers and for holidays. As Henry Cowell added to his land holdings, the home ranch eventually grew to 12,000 acres. In 1912, Overland Monthly published an article by Josephine McCracken about the Cowell family, which included a picture of the Cowell ranch house. [23]

After Isaac Davis died in 1888, Henry Cowell purchased his share of the business.[24] He renamed it Henry Cowell and Company, later renaming it the Henry Cowell Lime and Cement Company. Henry not only ran the lime and cement business, he kept busy acquiring land. At their most extensive, the Cowell holdings stretched from Texada Island in Canada down the coast to San Luis Obispo. Most of this land was acquired by Henry.

Henry Cowell avoided all publicity; as a result, little is known of him and his family. What is known is that Henry and his wife, Harriet, had five children, three girls, Isabella, Sarah and Helen, and two boys, Ernest and Samuel Henry (known as Harry or S. H.). Of the children, only Ernest married. Supposedly, their father "wouldn't allow boys coming around the house at all."[25] The children all attended Bay View school in Santa Cruz. Little is known of Henry's wife, Harriet. However Ernest Otto recalled seeing the Cowell family driving to the First Congregational Church each Sunday.[26]

Henry and Harriet Cowell in their carriage at the Cowell Home Ranch. The Carriage House, which today houses administrative offices on the campus of UC Santa Cruz, can be seen in the background. Date of photograph is unknown, but it was probably taken in the late 1800s. (Special Collections, University Library, UC Santa Cruz)

When Henry died in 1903, the company passed to his four surviving children: Ernest, Harry, Isabella and Helen. Sarah had died earlier that same year after being thrown from a runaway buggy. After their father's death Ernest took over management of the

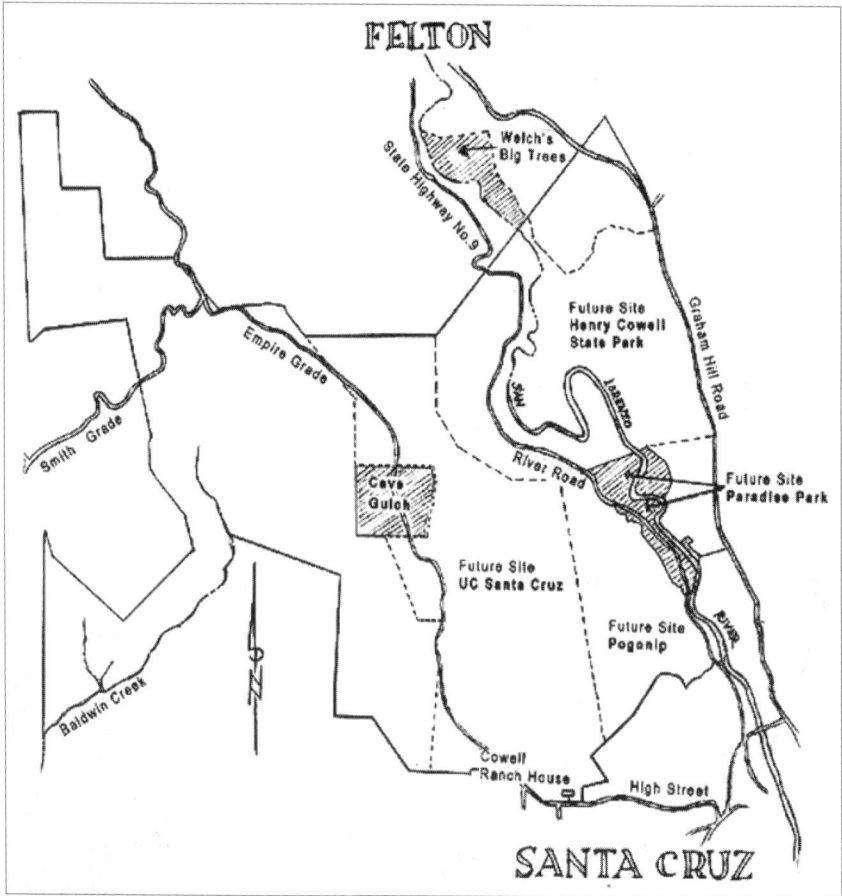

Approximately 6,500 acres of contiguous parcels made up part of the 12,000-acre Cowell Home Ranch. (The remaining parcels were further north and included the site of what is now Fall Creek State Park.) The Cowell Ranch House still stands just off High Street on the UC Santa Cruz property. The small portion of Pogonip between the San Lorenzo River and Highway 9 became the Sycamore Grove resort in the first half of the twentieth century. Cowell did not own the square section on Empire Grade (later the Cave Gulch subdivision) nor the parcel along the San Lorenzo River where the California Powder Works was located and which is now Paradise Park.

(Adapted from 1961 Plat of Cowell Foundation lands, Map Room, University Library, UCSC)

business. In the 1890s he moved to Tacoma, Washington to manage a branch office of the business there. Cement having proved far superior to lime as a building material, he built a large cement plant in Contra Costa County. Unfortunately, he was not able to manage the family business for long. Ernest died in 1911 at the age of 53, leaving an estate estimated to be worth more than one million dollars.

Upon Ernest's death, Harry took control of the family business. He was more interested in raising livestock than in the lime business. As ranch manager George Cardiff put it, "He was a cattleman. The other fellows were altogether lime." For a while Harry Cowell experimented with purebred bulls and he was reputed to own the finest racehorses in the state.[27] Perhaps it was because of his interest in horses that Harry Cowell was persuaded in 1935 to lease over 600 acres of his land to the Pogonip Polo Club.

The three surviving family members, Harry, Isabella, and Helen lived together in various combinations in the family homes in San Francisco and Atherton. Helen died in 1932 at the age of 66. After her death, Harry moved into the Cowell mansion in San Francisco with Isabella. She lived for another eighteen years, dying in 1950 at the age of 92. When Harry died in 1955 at the age of 93, he was the last of his family. Before he died, he established the S. H. Cowell Foundation to manage the Cowell estate.

Harry Cowell was known to care both for the welfare of his employees and for the welfare of his land. Because he wanted to preserve the redwoods on the Cowell property, he created in 1953 the 1,732-acre Henry Cowell Redwoods State Park on the San Lorenzo River near Felton. As a condition of his gift, he persuaded the state to acquire from the county, as centerpiece of the new state park, the Big Trees County Park (formerly Welch's Big Trees Resort), one of the oldest and finest stands of redwoods known to exist.[28] When Harry Cowell died, the Foundation that bears his name carried on his tradition of philanthropy.

The S. H. Cowell Foundation supported many charities throughout the state, and in the beginning, being richer in land than in cash, the foundation sold property to support these charities. In 1961 they sold the western portion of the Cowell Home Ranch to the regents of the University of California[29]; and in 1989 they sold the portion of the ranch known as Pogonip to the City of Santa Cruz to be preserved as open space.

Brochure touting the Santa Cruz recreational facilities, featuring the Golf and Country Club, issued by the Southern Pacific Railroad.
(Colleen McInerney-Meagher collection)

Chapter Three

A Santa Cruz Golf Club

A Thriving Resort City

At the end of the nineteenth century, Santa Cruz had become a thriving city—the industrial and business heart of the area. The expansion of the lime and lumber industries required new means of transport and new sources of power. Entrepreneurs, such as Frederick Augustus Hihn, were busy paving the streets and investing in real estate. Fred Wilder Swanton[1] was a founding director of the Swanton & Clark Electric Light and Power Company, which introduced the first incandescent lighting to Santa Cruz.[2] These early businessmen built mansions and presided over an extensive social life.

After the turn of the century, tourism became a new industry. Resorts in the Santa Cruz Mountains and at the beach offered diversions such as dancing and concerts, croquet, tennis, boating, swimming, riding, and golf. Fred Swanton was the most visible of the many entrepreneurs who developed what later became the Santa Cruz Beach Boardwalk and Casino.[3]

In 1903, Swanton was a director and main promoter of the Santa Cruz Beach, Cottage & Tent City Corporation, which bought a bathhouse on the Santa Cruz main beach and, in 1904, built the Neptune Casino. (At this time the area was not called the Boardwalk.) When in June 1906, shortly after the big earthquake, the casino burned to the ground, Swanton erected a huge tent and business went on as usual in the tent casino throughout the season. In 1906, the Santa Cruz Beach Company was formed to rebuild the casino. Fred Swanton was the director-general, but John Martin, a wealthy backer with ties to New York and Boston, was president and the heaviest investor. Construction began in October of 1906. The new casino opened to much fanfare in June of 1907.[4]

In 1911, Fred Swanton negotiated for the Santa Cruz Beach Company to lease land from S. H. Cowell for a country club and golf links. John Martin financed the project with the Southern Pacific Railroad. John Martin was at that time also owner of the Union Traction Company, which ran a streetcar line throughout Santa Cruz.

A New Golf Club

The land for the new golf club was located to the west of the road to Big Trees and the San Lorenzo River, just north of the city limits. It was part of the old Cowell home ranch, in the so-called Pogonip area.[5] The club was associated with the Casa del Rey Hotel and was named the Casa del Rey Country Club and Golf Links. It would have eighteen holes and be touted as the finest course, not only in the area, but also in the whole country.[6]

E. O. McCormick, vice president of the Southern Pacific Railroad, came to Santa Cruz to approve the location—and approve it he did: "Never before have I seen such a fine, natural spot for the links." He continued with the promise, "The S. P. Co. can be counted on to

The Casa del Rey golf course in 1912. The house in the left background, which was built by E. O. McCormick of the Southern Pacific Railroad, burned down in the 1970s. (Colleen McInerney-Meagher collection)

22

advertise the Santa Cruz links thoroughly throughout the country." The Southern Pacific officials planned a special station on the Southern Pacific Railroad, the Links Station, which allowed those arriving by train to get off at the Club and, after playing a round of golf, to be driven to the Casa del Rey hotel. Golfers could also take the morning train out from Santa Cruz, play for the day, and return on the evening train. The station itself was a flag stop, that is the train stopped only if the engineer saw passengers waiting or if the conductor signaled that people on board wanted to get off.[7]

E. O. McCormick was so taken with the beauty of the Casa del Rey golf course that in 1912 he built a vacation home at the top of the meadow overlooking the links. The estate, built on land leased from Cowell, included a swimming pool, extensive gardens and road access. The nearby rainwater cistern had a capacity of 14,000 gallons.[8]

Water was not a problem on this land. A spring gushed forth more than 150,000 gallons during the dry season, enough to provide continuous irrigation for the fairways as well as water for the clubhouse. A road was built from the county road, going under the Southern Pacific tracks, and cutting its way to the top of the hill where the clubhouse would stand. The view from the clubhouse site was spectacular.

Tom Bendelow of Chicago was hired to plan the golf course. He was an expert with the A. G. Spaulding Company and was recommended by E. O. McCormick. At that time, Bendelow was also laying out links in San Mateo, San Leandro, Stockton, Fresno, Bakersfield, and San Francisco, where he worked on the municipal course at Lincoln Park.[9] Mr. Bendelow gave lavish praise to the Santa Cruz setting:

"Here is one spot where nature intended that some day there should be a golf course. She formed these rolling benches and covered them with natural turf; then she made the protecting hills; and last, but not least, she made to burst forth from the hillside the wonderful Pogonip Spring, that always there should be a copious supply of pure, sweet water."[10]

Bendelow designed an interesting course. The first nine holes were 3,030 yards and the second nine 3,185 yards with a par of 73. In an article he wrote for the *Santa Cruz Surf*, he described each hole, even naming the 7th hole "El Purgatorio." He ended by saying, "Not a green is level, they all undulate, and as they are all sub-irrigated, the grass will be green the entire year."[11]

Design of the new Casa del Rey golf links. The first hole started at the top of a path that led up from the Links Station of the SP Railroad. The eighteenth hole ended in front of the clubhouse. The road to Santa Cruz Big Trees is what is now Highway 9; Pogonip Avenue is Golf Club Road. (Adapted from map in *Santa Cruz Sentinel*, February 22, 1912)

The Santa Cruz architect Lee Dill Esty was chosen to design the clubhouse "to be a roomy and rustic one-story bungalow" with an attic and basement. When built it would have a second story with a balcony overlooking the course.[12] An article in the *Santa Cruz Surf* describes how, from this balcony, one could look north, south, and west over almost every hole on the course, over the forested canyon of the San Lorenzo River to the City of Santa Cruz in the distance and the bay and ocean beyond. The eighteenth hole of the course was right in front of the clubhouse. In those days, the markers were not flags but tall poles.[13]

"The clubhouse itself is an attractive and well arranged structure, including two large rooms at either end of the building in which are lockers and baths for the men and women players. The main room

24

The clubhouse showing the marker for the eighteenth hole at the left. (Special Collections, University Library, UC Santa Cruz)

downstairs, into which you enter from the front door is immense in size and will be heated by the fires that will crackle and sputter in the big stone fireplace immediately across the room from the door. A kitchen, buffet and upstairs sleeping quarters for the help are other necessary rooms of the clubhouse."[14]

The Casa del Rey management sent out personal invitations to prominent citizens offering membership at a reduced rate. Eager to enlist members and not satisfied with personal invitations, the Casa del Rey management also put a public notice in the local newspaper.

Their efforts were successful. By February 17, 1912, the club had enlisted almost one hundred members, not counting members who signed up in San Francisco. The list of members included Fred Swanton and his wife, John Martin, S. H. Cowell, H. S. Deming and his family, the Lloyd Bowmans, the Frank Wilson family, the E. O. McCormicks, Samuel Leask, and F. A. Hihn, who bought six memberships in his own name. At that time, Charles B. Younger, despite his personal invitation, was not listed as a member. The list kept growing. As of February 22, 1912, over one hundred and thirty local people had applied to join the club.[15]

CASA DEL REY
GOLF AND COUNTRY CLUB
SANTA CRUZ, CALIFORNIA

Mr. _Chas B. Younger_

YOUR NAME HAS BEEN PROPOSED FOR MEMBERSHIP IN ABOVE NAMED CLUB.

THE CHARTER MEMBERSHIP HAS BEEN PLACED AT $10, AND WILL BE OPEN UNTIL FEBRUARY 20, AFTER WHICH DATE IT WILL BE INCREASED TO $25 OR MORE.

THE MONTHLY DUES WILL BE $3. FOR MEN AND $2. FOR LADIES.

THE MEMBERSHIP FEE $10.00 AND QUARTERLY DUES WILL BE DUE AND PAYABLE ON OR BEFORE FEBRUARY 20th 1912.

ENCLOSED FIND APPLICATION BLANK WHICH KINDLY FILL OUT AND FORWARD AT ONCE.

WE WISH TO ANNOUNCE THAT THE NEW GOLF LINKS WILL BE FORMALLY OPENED TO CLUB MEMBERS AND TO VISITORS ON WASHINGTON'S BIRTHDAY FEBRUARY 22, BY A CHAMPIONSHIP GOLF TOURNEY AND CONTINUING THROUGH THE BALANCE OF THE WEEK, ENDING SUNDAY, FEBRUARY 25, 1912.

A WEEKS PROGRAM OF ENTERTAINMENT HAS BEEN ARRANGED, WITH A GRAND BALL ON THE NIGHT OF WASHINGTON'S BIRTHDAY, AND SATURDAY EVENING, CONCERTS EVERY DAY, ELECTRICAL ILLUMINATIONS AND FIREWORKS EVERY NIGHT DURING TOURNEY.

CASA DEL REY MANAGEMENT

Invitation sent to Charles B. Younger by the Casa del Rey management. (Younger Papers Box 14 - MS 059, Special Collections, University Library, UC Santa Cruz)

Membership Application to the Casa del Rey Golf and Country Club, from the *Santa Cruz Surf*, February 5, 1912. (Seaside Company Archives)

Grand Opening

The new club opened in 1912 with a three-day golf tournament starting on Thursday, February 22 with the final matches played on Saturday, the 24th. Golfers arrived by automobile and railroad. Guests staying at the Casa del Rey Hotel in town were shuttled to the course by a four-in-hand that left every hour, starting at eight in the morning. Cars were also available to shuttle golfers between the Casa del Rey hotel and the links for fifty cents a round trip. The new club was promoted as a "working man's golf course with reasonable rates."[16]

The club management spared no expense. They imported twenty-five caddies for the use of their guests because the local caddies were not experienced enough to cater to the good golfers they expected. To keep the fairways trimmed, they brought in a flock of a thousand sheep with a Basque sheepherder to tend them.[17]

A 1912 article in the Surf describes a fish pond by the clubhouse, which was to be stocked with 250,000 trout to be "built and controlled by eight men and these rights will carry fishing privileges." The eight men included E. O. McCormick, John Martin, and Fred Swanton. In an earlier article in the Sentinel, Fred Swanton claimed he "stocked the creek with trout for the hotel … all fish caught must be cooked and eaten in the [Casa del Rey] hotel."[18]

The clubhouse in 1912. (Postcard, Colleen McInerney-Meagher collection)

27

The opening celebration began on the night preceding the tournament with a bandstand concert in front of the Casino, followed by fireworks from the pier, and culminated in a Washington's Birthday ball. Guests came from Monterey, Berkeley, Oakland, and other nearby towns, as well as from as far away as Chicago and New York.

Tournaments were held throughout the years and prominent Santa Cruz families played in them. Among those were G. H. Normand, Fred Swanton, Eulice Hihn (Frederick Augustus Hihn's grandson), and Henry S. Deming. Deming, a local banker, was the father of Dorothy Deming Wheeler who would in 1935 found the Pogonip Polo Club on the site of the Casa del Rey golf club. In a tournament in August of 1912, a young Miss Dorothy Deming won the junior golf finals by defeating Miss Violet Whitney.

Collage made from brochure for the new Casa del Rey Country Club and Golf Links. (Colleen McInerney-Meagher collection)

Donal' come brang the caddie,
I'll play g o l f wi' the stroke o' a mon,
Th' tell me these links at Santa Cruz
Are the finest for winnin' ones or twos
Outside o' our links in Scotlan'.

BIG TOURNEY ON AT THE LINKS

The golf tournament opened on Casa Del Rey links Thursday with a good attendance and weather that was grand. Many prominent people were present, including Vice-President McCormick of the Southern Pacific and party.

He arrived early in the morning in his special car and in order to be on hand for the first put was obliged to come in trailing onto a freight train.

Among the golf experts who played were the following: V. Whitney, Dr. Fredericks, Percy Selby, George Parsons, Cyril Tobin, Knox Maddox and M. Spencer, all of San Francisco. Considering the fact that not any of the seasoned players who entered Thursday morning are at all familiar with the links, except Dr. Fredericks, the scores made were very good.

The scores of the players in the men's qualifying round, 18 holes, medal play was as follows, the first sixteen winning places in the match for the championship, while the others will play for separate cups:

	Total	Ha'icap	Net
Dr. D. P. Fredericks	91	0	91
B. F. Chapman	91	15	76
F. A. Wilkins	92	12	80
W. F. Crist	94	15	79
Cyril Tobin	94	4	90
G. H. Normand	99	14	85
H. B. Palmer	100	10	90
Vincent Whitney	101	2	99
R. M. Kelly	102	18	84
M. Spencer	110	16	74
C. A. Belden	110	14	96
P. T. Prater	111	15	96
Mr. Turner	112	14	98
George Parsons	113	12	101
Percy Selby	114	12	102
R. J. Davis	114	14	100
C. F. Lilly	115	20	95
Knox Maddox	116	20	95
L. A. Redman	116	20	96
John Leonard	119	20	99
L. Bowman	122	25	97
M. Sharpe	129	25	104
H. Kron	131	18	112
Eulice Hihn	134	30	104
D. D. Curry	139	30	109
P. P. Bliss	140	25	115
Fred Swanton	141	20	121
G. L. Grant	155	30	125
H. F. Irish	160	20	140
Capt. Dorcey	161	20	141

WOMEN'S SCORES:

	Total	Ha'icap	Net
Miss Warner	110	0	110
Mrs. Warner	132	10	122
Mrs. Graves	142	15	127
Mrs. Linscott	161	20	141
Mrs. E. Hihn	186	20	148
Mrs. Wilson	183	20	163
Mrs. Thorburn	191	20	171
Mrs. F. Hihn	192	20	172
Mrs. J. Scott	200	20	180
Mrs. J. Scott	200	20	180
Mrs. Rittenhouse	200	20	180
Mrs. Dalton	205	20	185

The new course must have been difficult judging by the scores of the contestants.
(Colleen McInerney-Meagher collection)

29

Golfers practicing by the Casa del Rey Golf and Country Club clubhouse. This putting green was subsequently paved over to be the parking lot for the Pogonip Polo Club. (Colleen McInerney-Meagher collection)

Clubhouse and pond. Notice the hole marker to the right of the clubhouse and the putting green in front of the clubhouse. The pond in the foreground was perhaps the fish pond promised by Fred Swanton. (Special Collections, UC Santa Cruz)

Financial Trouble

Shortly after the new club opened to great fanfare, a number of events occurred that were to make its future problematic. In 1912 Fred Swanton declared bankruptcy forcing the club to reorganize as the Santa Cruz Golf and Country Club. (The officers of the newly renamed club were: William T. Jeter, president; Henry S. Deming, vice president; and Edgar M. Wilson, secretary/treasurer.) Then, the so-called "Taft Depression" cut into the number of people who had money for visits to the beach and to play golf. Finally, in 1915, the financially troubled Santa Cruz Beach Company was taken over by the Santa Cruz Seaside Company.[19]

By 1917 the golf club was in serious financial trouble. In April of 1917, the *Santa Cruz Surf* reported that the club fees had been dropped to $2.50 a month and the usual entrance charge eliminated. This would, the article said, "place the links at the disposal of many who would not care to pay the usual entrance charge." By the following week, the *Surf* reported that 126 new members had been enrolled and that more would be enrolled shortly.[20]

In 1919 the club was still in trouble. And it was becoming more and more difficult to maintain the links. The local newspapers published pleas for new members. To potential local members, they praised the location so near to downtown, and to out-of-towners, they pointed out its ease of access by train or by car and the low fees.[21]

New Design

In 1922, a golf expert, W. Locke, associated with the San Francisco golf club, proposed a general remodeling of the links. This seems to have occurred (perhaps when a new sprinkler system was installed).[22] The undated map of the redesigned course is significantly different from the original Tom Bendelow design. In that earlier design, the first nine holes encircled the second nine holes. In the new design, the first nine holes are on the lower bench of the land; the second nine holes are on the upper bench; and the eighteenth hole is no longer directly in front of the clubhouse.

The club was featured in the 1923-1924 edition of Green Book of Golf.[23] The yardages shown in the book differ only slightly from those on the map of the redesigned course, perhaps the result of a slight tweaking between design and implementation. The course is

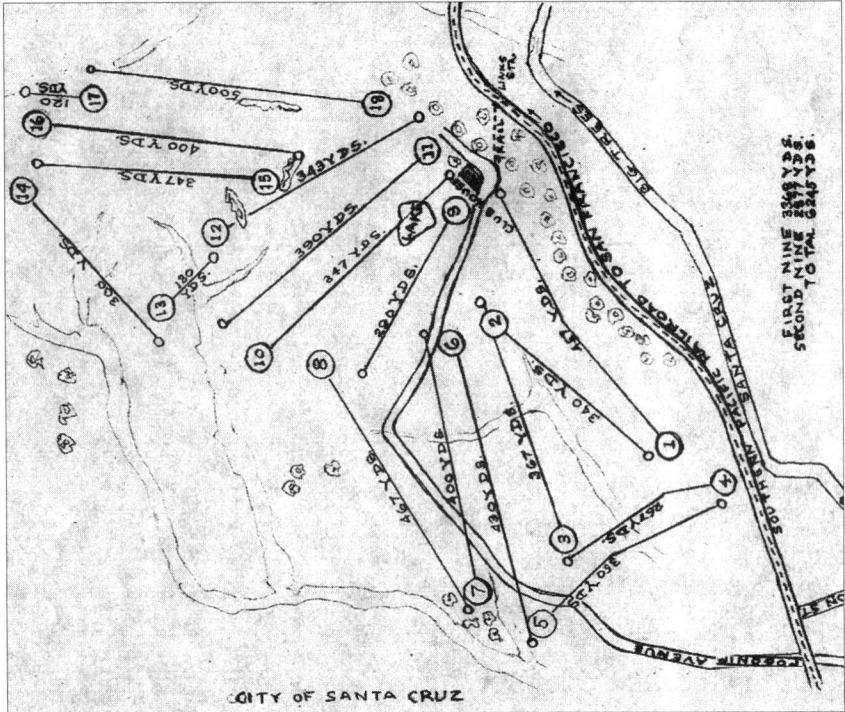

The redesigned golf links. (Map Room, University Library, UC Santa Cruz)

still par 73. At this time Bob Jones was president and had been, apparently, living at the links in the McCormick house.[24]

With a modern water system and redesigned links, the club seemed to thrive. These were the boom times of the 1920s. In 1928, the *Santa Cruz Evening News* wrote a promotional article stating that the course was in good shape with links that "are regarded as the best natural layout in this section of the state."[25]

However at the end of 1929, the Santa Cruz chamber of commerce voted to ask the city to include financial aid for the course in their budget for the coming year. The club had borrowed $4,000 to help pay the $10,000 cost of the new water system. This loan had been endorsed by various members and by the Seaside Company. At least ten of the local backers of the club offered to cancel the $1,000 in notes they held against the club. Among them was William T. Jeter who returned his note to the club marked "Cancelled."[26]

In December of 1929, the club president, Robert L. Cardiff, and David L. Wilson, chairman of the golf committee, went to San Francisco to confer with the Henry Cowell Lime and Cement

Company regarding the future of the club. The Company responded with an offer to lower the rent for one year from $300 to $150 per month, subject to improvements by the club. The club requested three years to make the extensive improvements and Cowell accepted.[27]

Santa Cruz Golf and Country Club

OFFICERS

President	Bob Jones
Vice-President	D. L. Wilson
Secretary	W. H. Normand

DIRECTORS

Henry Willey   Morris Abrams   H. E. Irish

D. L. Wilson   Bob Jones

C. J. Klein   C. H. Griffen, Jr.

CHAIRMAN HOUSE COMMITTEE
D. L. Wilson

CHAIRMAN FIELDS AND SPORTS COMMITTEE
C. H. Griffen, Jr.

GOLF PROFESSIONAL
Al. Abrego

CARD OF THE LINKS

Hole	Yards	Par	Hole	Yards	Par
1	462	5	10	354	4
2	223	3	11	377	4
3	302	4	12	299	4
4	142	3	13	129	3
5	317	4	14	253	4
6	478	5	15	476	5
7	587	4	16	466	5
8	447	5	17	121	3
9	355	4	18	443	4
Out	3,113	37	In	2,918	36
			Out	3,113	37
			Total	6,031	73

A page reproduced from the 1923-1924 edition of "The Green Book of Golf" describing the Santa Cruz Golf and Country Club in 1923. Notice that the course is par 73.

The improvements, however, turned out to be expensive. Reseeding the fairways, installing new pipes and a new sprinkler system meant they had to raise $7,500. To do this they needed a membership of 300. The club went ahead and made as many improvements as they could afford. Enrollment went up to over 200 but it was still not enough.

Final Days

The prosperous days of the 1920s had ended. Even before the stock market crash of 1929, the Santa Cruz club could no longer boast the best golf course in the region. On September 2, 1929, Marion Hollins had opened her superb new Pasatiempo course. Then in 1930, Rio Del Mar in Aptos opened another 18-hole course. The competition was overwhelming.

By February of 1933, the club was down to 11 members, not all of them paid up. In April, local businessmen were still meeting with the Henry Cowell Lime and Cement Company to try to revive the now dormant club, but to no avail. By 1934, the Santa Cruz Golf and Country Club had closed and, in closing, opened up a golden opportunity for a new club to take over its location, its turf, and its water—but for polo, not golf.[28]

Polo was fast becoming an important Santa Cruz sport. Starting in the early 1920s, local polo players were busy forming leagues and trying to develop a world-class polo field. That dream would be realized when Dorothy Deming Wheeler and her husband Deming Wheeler opened the Pogonip Polo Club in 1936 on the site of the old Santa Cruz Golf and Country Club.

Chapter Four

Dorothy Deming Wheeler

Early Life

Dorothy Deming Wheeler, the guiding force behind the formation of the Pogonip Polo Club, was a resident of Santa Cruz, California, from early childhood. Born January 24, 1895, in Los Gatos, she moved with her family to Santa Cruz when she was three years old. Dorothy's father, Henry Seth Deming, was a wealthy banker, originally from Terre Haute, Indiana. Her mother Josephine was a native of Pana, Illinois but had lived in Santa Cruz prior to her marriage. Coming to California in the 1890s, Henry Deming moved his young family to Santa Cruz in 1897. There, he built a grand Eastlake Victorian mansion for his family on fashionable Beach Hill. They moved into the house as soon as it was completed in 1899.

Their home, Deming House, was 13,500 square feet and included a ballroom on the top floor. A separate carriage house had a caretaker's apartment upstairs. Deming House still stands on Beach Hill.[1] Although the inside of the structure has been divided into apartments, the well-maintained exterior reflects the mansion's former glory.

In later years, Dorothy reminisced about the old days on Beach Hill. She told of going down to the beach in a horse-drawn cart. She said, "It'd drive right out into the surf and we'd jump in the waves. Later, families set up brightly colored tents and I remember my mother serving tea in ours. It was rather exclusive." That was a time when almost all transportation was by horse and carriage. Later, the family owned an automobile, a white Stanley Steamer. It was probably one of the first cars in town and was driven by a chauffer named Leo.[2]

Dorothy Deming Wheeler in front in front of the fireplace at Windy Hill Farm, the mantel by that time filled with trophies won by women on the polo field. The fireplace screen is inset with a copper replica of a photo of Deming Wheeler. (Colleen McInerney-Meagher collection)

Sidebar

Deming House Restored

Located at 417 Cliff Street, the Eastlake Victorian was designed by Edward L. Van Cleeck and built for H. S. Deming between 1895 and 1899. The home's top floor was a ballroom with a soaring 27-foot ceiling of redwood beams. In 1995, Deming House was bought and lovingly restored by Matt Greenberg.

Once one of the grandest homes in Santa Cruz, it had over the years been divided into apartments and fallen into disrepair through a horde of tenants.

One room at a time, Greenberg stripped layers of paint off the hardwood floors, refurbished original light fixtures and restored the redwood trim. The grand old home is now divided into six apartments and the carriage house into four studio apartments. The largest apartment, 2,300 square feet, comes complete with the upstairs ballroom.

The restoration is a mix of old and new; the plumbing, electrical fixtures and appliances are new, while the claw-foot tubs, old toilets, ironing boards built into the walls, and stamped tin ceilings have been kept. [3]

Dorothy led the life of a privileged young lady of the early twentieth century. Her early school days were spent at the Laurel School in Santa Cruz, where her classmates were children of the Stagnaro, Bliss, Jeter, and Wilder families.[4] (The old Laurel School was where the Louden Nelson center is today.) Later she went away to boarding school, graduating from Miss Ransom's School for Girls in Piedmont, California.

Dorothy grew up to be a large-boned handsome woman who excelled in sports, learning to ride horses at a young age. She was also accomplished at golf and tennis. She was a doubles partner of Helen Wills Moody of Wimbledon fame and she played with the United States women's tennis champion, Fay Sutton.

Marriage

When Dorothy was around nineteen years old, she met Deming Wheeler. Almost twenty years Dorothy's senior, Deming was from the Terre Haute, Indiana, branch of Dorothy's family. Deming Wheeler was born August 23, 1877 in Brattleboro, Vermont. His father was Brigadier General Daniel Davis Wheeler, a congressional medal winner in the Civil War. The Wheeler family later moved to Terre Haute, Indiana, where they became important citizens. His mother was the former Sophie Deming of Terre Haute, sister of Henry S. Deming, Dorothy's father. Thus Dorothy and Deming were first cousins.[5]

World traveler, big-game hunter, polo player, and a world-renowned authority on breeding strains of dogs and horses. Deming was a dapper man. He made his presence felt as he strode into a room in his freshly pressed gabardine suits, his felt hat banded by a grosgrain ribbon and his waxed moustache curled at the ends. Just under six feet tall, the balance of his step showed the athletic ability acquired through years of riding and training horses. A sportswoman herself, it is easy to understand young Dorothy's attraction to him.

Deming had a terrific reputation as a polo player. He got his nickname of "Cannon Ball Wheeler" when he played polo on Long Island. "When he had the line of the ball, so they said, he went straight for the goal. And even sometimes when he didn't have the line."[6]

Dorothy and Deming wished to marry. Her family, however, was adamantly opposed to the marriage. They had a number of reasons: her age, his age, and the fact that they were first cousins. Eventually,

Deming "Cannonball" Wheeler on Cha Cha in the 1920s. This is the photo reproduced on the fire screen at Windy Hill. (Colleen McInerney-Meagher collection)

however, Dorothy's parents gave in to their daughter's wishes, and at three in the afternoon on the 28th of August in 1916, they were married in the Deming mansion on Beach Hill. Dorothy was twenty-one years old and Deming was thirty-nine.

The wedding was simple, attended only by her immediate family and by Deming's mother, Mrs. Sarah Sophie Deming Wheeler, who was also Dorothy's aunt. Dorothy wore a gown "of army blue trimmed with natural lynx with hat en suite."[7] Fur trim on dresses was quite the latest thing at that time and a non-white wedding gown, particularly one in a military color, was not uncommon during World War I.[8] The ceremony took place in the flower-filled music room of the mansion followed by a wedding supper in the dining room. Immediately afterwards, the bride and groom left for Seattle and then for Fairbanks, Alaska, where they spent their honeymoon.[9]

Thus it was that in her home, surrounded by family, Dorothy Deming became Dorothy Deming Wheeler, entering into a marriage that lasted until Deming's death in 1946. The newlyweds' honeymoon in Alaska, an exotic and non-traditional destination, particularly in the early 1900s, set the tone of their marriage. On their honeymoon, Dorothy and Deming took a thousand-mile dog sled journey from Fairbanks to Nome and back, with Dorothy driving her own team of ten to thirteen dogs. This sojourn in Alaska showed

Dorothy a whole new vision of what life could be like. From now on she and Deming would be partners in an unconventional marriage filled with sports and adventure.

While they were in Alaska in the winter of 1917-1918, Dorothy learned her father was ill. She rushed home to find that he had already died on January 4, 1918.[10] His body had been kept in a vault to await her arrival before the burial in Oakland. Her mother died five years later in March of 1923.[11] At that time Dorothy was living in Santa Cruz and was able to be with her mother when she died.

Windy Hill Farm

In the early 1920s, the Wheelers purchased an 80-acre parcel of land in Santa Cruz at the top of Spring Street, adjoining the land that would become Pogonip. There they built a house, designed by Noble Newsom, in the style of an English country manor. The house was completed in May of 1921. Calling it Windy Hill Farm, Deming set up a ranch for dog and horse breeding.[12]

Soon after it was built, in January of 1922, the house at Windy Hill Farm burned down. The road to their house had not been passable to fire equipment, so the firemen were unable to save the home. The Wheelers were able to salvage only a few valuables, including some prized relics, and most of the doors and windows.[13] Undismayed, Deming swore they would rebuild the house on the same site and began erecting a guest house on the property where they could live during construction of their new home. He also made significant improvements to the private road leading up to his property—never again would fire trucks be unable to reach his house.[14]

Farm House at Windy Hill after it was rebuilt. (Colleen McInerney-Meagher collection)

Three of the young men who helped train the ponies at Windy Hill Farm; from the left: Budd Kann, Bill Whitney, and Perry Pond in the stable doorway.
(Colleen McInerney-Meagher collection)

When the Wheelers rebuilt the house on Spring Street in 1929, they put down brick floors in the hallway of the house and installed an oversized copper clad door; this allowed Deming to bring his horses into the house so he could show them to his invalid mother, Sophie Deming Wheeler, who lived with them in her later years.

At the same time, they put on a new tile roof that, according to the news accounts of the day, weighed almost 30 tons. The tile was hand made, each tile hand colored and individually baked. Thick and rough and softly colored, it gave the effect of age, which was enhanced by laying the tile in broken lines and irregular projections; the resulting effect was most pleasing.[15] It was also fire proof.

The former Windy Hill Farm is now subdivided into a residential housing development accessible only through a gated entrance. The English country-manor style house still stands but is surrounded by other houses.

Besides raising horses and dogs, the Wheelers kept other livestock: poultry, particularly ducks and geese for eggs and meat, as well as goats for milk and cheese and also for meat. They maintained two acres of a practical garden where they raised fruits and vegetables for the table. The horses, however, were their primary interest.[16]

Bill Whitney, horse trainer *par excellence*, on Deming Wheeler's breeding stallion, Ortolan, in front of the stables at Windy Hill Farm.
(Colleen McInerney-Meagher collection)

Deming Wheeler's thoroughbred horses were sold to polo players around the world. In 1937, Dorothy reported proudly that, after ten years of breeding, the first colts they had sent to market were being played in Long Island, England, India, Africa, and Honolulu. She noted, however that, "The actual sums paid for these horses would not go very far in paying the expenses of their breeding and training."[17] Bob Gillies, who was a groom at Windy Hill in those days, recalls that he heard it cost between $3,000 and $3,500 a month to run the stables. This cost was exclusive of the Wheeler's personal living expenses.[18]

In the early days of their marriage, Dorothy learned to play polo with Deming on a dirt, or "skinned," field in Santa Cruz. Her playing improved when they went to Santa Barbara in the spring and summer to play on the good fast fields there. As her polo playing improved, she and Deming became more and more interested in developing a good field nearer home. Soon they were in the forefront of bringing polo to Santa Cruz.

Chapter Five

Polo Comes To Santa Cruz

Early Polo Fields

The future development of Pogonip came about because the polo players of Santa Cruz wanted a world-class polo field. In the early 1920s, California boasted a number of fine polo fields: the Del Monte, San Mateo, and San Francisco fields in the North; the Bartlett, Cox, and Fleischmann fields in Santa Barbara; and the fields at Midwick and the Will Rogers ranch in the South. But Santa Cruz had no field on which its increasingly dedicated polo players could practice their game.

Then, in 1922, a group of avid local players began to meet out at the Wilder ranch north of town on Sunday afternoons for informal games. In addition to Melvin and Deloss Wilder, the ranch owners, these players included Deming and Dorothy Wheeler, Sam Leask, Jr., of local department store fame, Frank G. Wilson of Wilson Brothers Realty, and physician Dr. Golden "Goldie" Falconer.[1]

In these early games, Dorothy Wheeler played right along with the men. At that time she was the only woman playing in coed games in the West. She was, however, setting a precedent that would soon be followed by many of her daring colleagues, women who first joined men's teams and then started teams of their own.

The Wilders only dabbled in polo. Being more interested in cattle roping and rodeos, they saw no need to improve their polo grounds, and the games at the Wilder ranch were either very muddy or very dusty, depending on the Santa Cruz season. So the Wheelers, Sam Leask, the Wilsons, and Goldie Falconer got together to finance a field dedicated to polo.

Bay and California Polo Field

In July of 1923, the polo aficionados proudly opened a new polo field at the corner of Bay and California Avenues on the west side of Santa Cruz near Neary Lagoon. This field, though less than regulation size, was in a splendid location close to the center of the city and near to streetcar lines.[2] Soon the new field was the center of much activity. The local teams held practice sessions on weekday afternoons, and had regular competitive games on weekends. Pleased with their new polo grounds, the players made plans to challenge outside teams.

Sam Leask, Jr. was selected as captain of a team to represent Santa Cruz at the Del Monte midsummer tournament in Monterey. The Del Monte teams were mostly made up of military men stationed at the Monterey Presidio. In that tournament, the newly formed Santa Cruz team played a team from the Fortieth Infantry Regiment. The local paper boasted that the new field was "satisfactory in every respect."[3]

Soon, Santa Cruz added a second team to their line up, and they prepared to play teams from Stanford, Berkeley and the U. S. Army. The two Santa Cruz teams, the Juniors and Seniors, practiced by playing each other.[4] At the end of October, the Santa Cruz Senior team defeated the visiting Seventy-Sixth Artillery team so decisively (7-2) that they fielded their Junior team for the next game.[5]

That same October, Tom Mix, the cowboy star, was invited by the Polo Club to come up to Santa Cruz to play in an exhibition game. A large crowd was expected to come to see him play.[6] Polo had really hit the big time in the small town of Santa Cruz.

All in all, it seemed as if things were going well for the Santa Cruz players. But, now that they were expanding so successfully, they began to notice the drawbacks of the Bay/California field. It had no stables for horses and no clubhouse for members. Without

A Santa Cruz team defeating the 76th Field Artillery team at the Bay Street Field, October 1923. (Dorothy Deming Wheeler scrapbooks)

stables each player had to cart his or her horses to the field using special motorized vans carrying from three to six ponies. Without a clubhouse there was no place to gather after a match to celebrate their wins or mourn their losses. The Santa Cruz players started looking around for a new site.

Aptos Polo Field

The site of the old Spreckels racetrack in Aptos was picked as the location for a new polo field. The racetrack was an enormous flat space with room for a proper-sized field. It even had a run-down stable that could be repaired with a little effort and money. The oval area was a natural amphitheater surrounded by trees growing on a gentle slope along its long sides. Up to 500 cars could be parked beside the field for spectators. The *Evening News* claimed, "The scope and natural beauty of the field was a revelation in itself."[7]

Now that they had a polo field, the players had more ambitious plans. They founded the Aptos-Santa Cruz Polo Club to oversee the maintenance of the field and the building of stables and a clubhouse. The plan was to keep a large stable of polo ponies and riding horses at the club for the use of the club owners. By June of 1925, Harry Hastings and Ralph Spivalo, both well-known polo players, had joined the staff of the club.

At about this time, a trio of real estate developers, L.G. Monroe,

Aptos Polo Field, 1924. A game with the 11th Cavalry. Notice the dust in front of the cars parked behind the sideboards. (Colleen McInerney-Meagher collection)

"Beauty and the Beast and Polo" From an announcement of Wilson Brothers & Associates, Inc. Realtors. The photo shows Miss Los Angeles, here for the Miss California pageant, holding the bridle of "Brownie" ridden by Frank G. Wilson with Sam Leask, Jr. on the far right, at the Aptos Polo Field in the 1920s. (Photo by William H. Sherer, courtesy of David Wilson of Wilson Brothers Realty.)

W. C. Lyon, and L. J. Miller, picked Aptos as the location for a new development, Rio Del Mar, to be marketed to Eastern golfers and polo players who wanted to escape harsh winters in a more temperate climate. The developers envisioned an Aptos Beach Country Club where golf and polo would be the major sports.

Monroe, Lyon, and Miller were pleased to find that a polo club already existed on the property they planned to develop. To win the support of the polo club, they made an offer to rebuild the stables, provide a modern club house for members, turf the polo field and supply an irrigation system, and allow the token rental of one dollar a year to continue for five years. They would remodel the ranch house on the Aptos Club property as headquarters for the Aptos-Santa Cruz Polo Club. The only catch in the grand plan was that the polo club had to have a charter membership of 200 people in order for Monroe, Lyon, and Miller to make these improvements.[8]

Time passed and polo playing at Aptos continued. Women frequently played with the men and the competitive coed games helped attract spectators.[9] By October of 1925, membership had grown to 185—still short of the magic number, now apparently raised to 250. So close to this goal, the club looked forward to making the needed improvements. They received bids for a clubhouse, a turf field that would be green year round, and a practice field above the regular field.[10]

For almost four years, the Aptos field remained a center for polo. Eventually, however, it became clear that the developers were not going to honor their commitment to pay for the cost of planting and maintaining a grass field. The Aptos field was a "skinned" field, the name given a dirt field, which made for slow and messy games. The top players they had hoped to lure to Aptos drifted away to play on grass fields in other places, such as Del Monte or Santa Barbara. As Deming Wheeler pointed out, "We cannot draw to the wonderful surroundings of the Aptos field the number of outside players we should like so long as they must endure clouds of dust. We have great hopes from the promises of Monroe, Lyon and Miller."[11] These hopes, however, were not to be realized.

In October of 1929, it was announced that the beautiful Aptos polo field would cease to exist. The money spent on turfing and water appliances was a total loss; the land was to be leased for the cultivation of strawberries.[12]

In 1927, disappointed by the drawbacks of the Aptos polo field, the Wheelers began taking their horses to play in Santa Barbara. After four years of trouble and expense carting their ponies south, the couple contemplated retiring from the game to settle down full-time to life at Windy Hill Farm. Then Marion Hollins came to town, bringing with her an energy and drive that, together with Dorothy Wheeler's focus and determination, resulted in a new polo field for Santa Cruz.

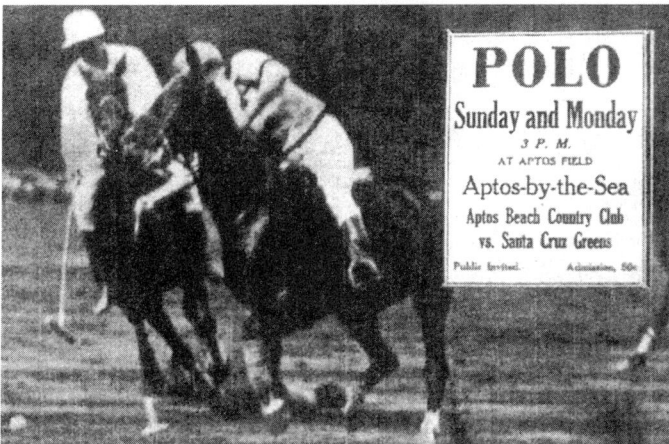

Announcement of a polo game at the Aptos Polo Field with photo of polo players reproduced in *The Aptos Almanac*. (Courtesy of Rob Doerr and the Aptos Museum)

POLO

Sunday and Monday
3 P. M.
AT APTOS FIELD

Aptos-by-the-Sea

Aptos Beach Country Club
vs. Santa Cruz Greens

Public Invited.   Admission, 50c

Marion Hollins Arrives in Santa Cruz

Marion Hollins was a wealthy sportswoman from Long Island and a top woman golfer. She was also an outstanding tennis player and horsewoman. She played polo on the North Shore of Long Island with the men's teams and in Aiken, South Carolina with Louise Hitchcock, an early advocate of women's polo.

Born to great wealth, Marion's early life was idyllic. Sports were central to the Hollins family life and Marion was an avid athlete, her abilities honed by competition with three sports-mad brothers. Her earliest interest was in horses and riding, but in her teen years, her full attention shifted to golf and she became a champion golfer. In 1921 she won the U. S. Women's National Amateur Championship.

Coming to California in 1924 as "athletic director" at Del Monte, she worked with the developer S. F. B. Morse to promote the area as a golfer's paradise. She became very successful in real estate, touting Pebble Beach and the joys of California life to her wealthy friends in the East. She went on to help develop Cypress Point, arguably the most beautiful and challenging golf course ever built.

In 1927, Marion traveled north to Santa Cruz looking for the perfect place on which to build another world-class course. One day, while riding in the hills above Santa Cruz, she fell in love with the land that was to become the golf and housing development she called *Pasatiempo*, Spanish for *pastime*. It was rolling land, broken by the wooded canyon of Carbonero Creek, with knolls and slopes dotted with oak trees and, in the very center, a vast stretch of open meadow. Seeing the land, Marion envisioned the great golf course she would build there.[13]

In December of 1927, Marion Hollins bought the land for Pasatiempo (around 570 acres) from Bertha Coope, the surviving daughter of F. W. Billing and his wife, Wilhelmina. Their home, Billing House, a large Victorian mansion, was located on the current site of the Pasatiempo Inn.[14] She then went back East to raise the money to develop the land and build her dream golf course.

Once Marion Hollins owned the land and had financial backing, she hired experts to advise her on the grand design for Pasatiempo. Marion was not able to realize all her plans for Pasatiempo at once— it was years before the polo field was built—but the golf course was a big success. Marion was intimately involved with the actual shaping of the Pasatiempo course and no trees were removed without her permission. By saving the live oaks she preserved the natural

Marion Hollins at Pasatiempo with Dagmar, the horse and Carlos, the dog. A 1933 Christmas card photo.
(Wilson Collection, Pasatiempo Golf Club)

beauty of the land and added to the interest of the course.

Marion went on to buy more property including 128 acres in Scotts Valley for a racetrack. She built the track and also a fabulous horse barn designed by William Wurster. In 1932, when Marion Hollins and Dorothy Wheeler got together, Marion was able to add a polo field to her Pasatiempo holdings on land she had acquired off Graham Hill Road.

Marion and Dorothy Bring Polo to Pasatiempo

As fellow polo players, it was only natural that Marion Hollins and Dorothy Wheeler should meet and become friends. The two women made an interesting pair. Both were about the same age, Marion being only three years older than Dorothy. Both were raised in wealthy families. Both were physically similar, being tall, large boned women. Both were outstanding athletes at a time when women were not expected to excel at sports. And they were both excellent polo players, as good as or better than many of the California men.

It was through their friendship—and a lucky chance—that the Pasatiempo polo field came into being. Marion and Dorothy had, on occasion, talked about building a new polo field on Marion's Pasatiempo property. This vague idea became a reality after a fluke bet at the Tanforan racetrack. One day in 1932, Marion and Dorothy went to the races together. Dorothy asked Marion to place a bet for her on horse Number 9. Marion accidentally placed the bet on Number 7, a lame horse that was not expected to make it around the track, let alone win a race. A very apologetic Marion reported to

Dorothy Deming Wheeler and Marion Hollins at Pasatiempo. Dorothy is holding the trophy won by the Pasatiempo women's team in a 1934 game with the Riviera women's team.
(Pasatiempo Archives)

Dorothy on her mistake. But, then in the upset of the day, the lame horse came in to win—paying $450 on the dollar. Dorothy had won a substantial amount of money on Marion's mistake. Dorothy later reported: "I tried to give my winnings to the lucky purchaser, but Marion wouldn't accept it. So, I leveled a little polo field instead."

Together, Marion Hollins and the Wheelers built a field. The Wheelers paid to have the Pasatiempo polo field leveled inside the oval racetrack off Graham Hill Road that Marion Hollins owned (later the Graham Hill Showgrounds). Marion built stables in Scotts Valley, the William Wurster polo barn, where the Wheelers kept some of their horses. The Wheelers paid for installing irrigation and, subsequently, for maintaining the field.

A Women's Polo Association

Now that Santa Cruz had a polo field to which they could invite visiting teams and a Pasatiempo women's polo team, Dorothy Wheeler got busy organizing all the polo-playing women of California into teams. In the process, she was instrumental in developing the United States Women's Polo Association, the first and only women's polo association ever to be formed in the United States.

In December of 1933 representatives from all the women's teams, including the newly formed Pasatiempo team, met in Los Angeles. Their purpose was to form a league of their own—a league that could hold tournaments and present trophies. Dorothy Wheeler did not go to this meeting; she was laid up with a badly broken arm. But she was there in spirit, keeping up with plans through a voluminous correspondence.

When the new Pacific Coast Women's Polo Association was formed in January of 1934, Dorothy was selected as its first president. Louise Tracy of the Riviera Club in Santa Monica was its first secretary-treasurer. (A few years later, in 1936, the women changed the association name to the United States Women's Polo Association.)

In November of 1934, the Pasatiempo women's polo team proudly hosted the first tournament of the newly formed Pacific Coast Women's Polo Association. A Pasatiempo team that included both Dorothy Wheeler and Marion Hollins defeated the Riviera women's team to win the perpetual trophy of the new association.

Good as the Pasatiempo field was in comparison to the previous Santa Cruz polo fields, it was not good enough to satisfy Dorothy Wheeler's high standards. The field was undersized and, because the grass they planted never took hold, it raised a lot of dust. Dorothy wanted a field that could proudly host the best players of the day, that would do honor to the new women's polo association she had formed, and that would provide women players the same facilities as the men. She would soon have that field at the newly formed Pogonip Polo Club.

A polo game on the Pasatiempo polo field in 1934. This was the best field yet—a field Santa Cruz could be proud of. (Colleen McInerney-Meagher collection)

Chapter Six

The Pogonip Polo Club

New Polo Field For Santa Cruz

In November of 1935, a local paper announced that "Rich Backers" had completed negotiations with "Henry Cowell" to take over the lease of the Santa Cruz Golf Club (formerly the Casa del Rey Country and Golf Club) from the Cowell organization. The lease was taken in the name of a new club, the Pogonip Polo Club.[1]

The lease was for much more land than had been leased by the Santa Cruz Golf Club. The Pogonip club was to have over 600 acres; the golf club had leased a mere 145 acres. The group who took out the lease were: Dorothy and Deming Wheeler; Robert Law, a polo-playing friend, his first wife, Jane, and his mother, Frances Law; and Harold Lane, another polo player. The Laws had moved to Santa

Bob Law with polo mallet between two men holding horses on the new Pogonip Polo Club field.
(Colleen McInerney-Meagher collection)

Cruz from New York when Frances Law bought a house at Pasatiempo and her daughter-in-law, Jane Law, bought Vine Hill Farm from their friend Marion Hollins. The Laws planned to breed horses at their new farm, renamed Lawridge.

The new site had many advantages: it was already completely piped with spring water; it was turfed with hard-wearing Bermuda grass—the ideal turf for polo as well as for golf; it had a beautiful clubhouse; and, perhaps best of all for the Wheelers, it was a short horse-back ride from their Windy Hill Farm. The Wheelers proceeded to have all the turf lifted from the upper fairway of the golf course, put aside while they leveled a regulation-sized polo field, and put back down to provide a superb surface for polo. The cost of developing the field was reported to be $12,000.[2]

On May 22, 1936, the Pogonip Polo Club was officially incorporated. In ensuing years many of the top polo players in the world would play on its superb new turf.

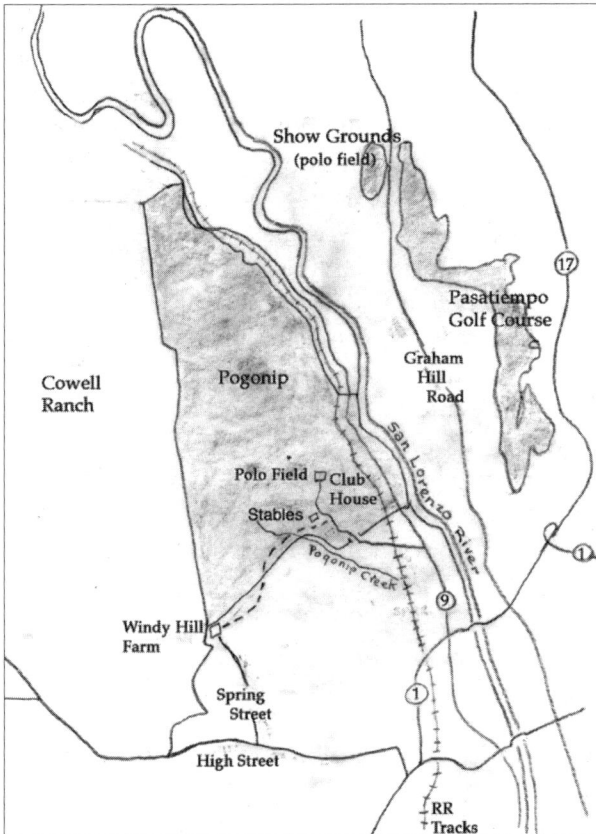

Pogonip Polo Club in relation to the Pasatiempo Golf Course and the old Pasatiempo Polo Field at Graham Hill Show Grounds. The route from Windy Hill Farm to Pogonip (shown with a dashed line) went through what was then undeveloped land, entered Pogonip near where Lookout Trail meets Pogonip Creek Trail today, forded Pogonip Creek, and continued past the stables up to the polo field and clubhouse.

Pasatiempo and Pogonip

When they opened their polo club, the Wheelers expected they would have two main polo fields, the new regulation field at Pogonip and the old dirt field at Pasatiempo. They assumed ownership of the Pasatiempo field on Graham Hill road and planned to use the Pasatiempo field in conjunction with the Pogonip field. It soon became clear that Dorothy planned not only to take over the Pasatiempo field but also to absorb the Pasatiempo team. She would do this by changing the name of the team from "Pasatiempo" to "Pogonip." She had already given cards to the Pasatiempo team members stating they were now members of the Pogonip team.[3] Dorothy did not directly inform Marion of this change nor, apparently, did she inform the association.

Marion, however, was not ready to let the Pasatiempo team be absorbed into the Pogonip fold. In a letter to the United States Women's Polo Association, Marion said, "Pasatiempo certainly intends to continue being a member of the association, and in fact, is going into polo in a far bigger way than before." The upshot was that Marion, gracious as ever, paid the dues for the Pasatiempo team and also paid the $75 fee to become a member of the new Pogonip Polo Club.[4] There were now two women's polo teams in Santa Cruz; one from the Pasatiempo Club with Marion Hollins at the helm and the other from Pogonip with Dorothy Wheeler in charge.

The disagreement between Marion Hollins and Dorothy Wheeler was not all one sided. Dorothy had good reasons for believing the Pasatiempo Polo team was hers. She had solicited many of the players on the Pasatiempo team and she was responsible for paying the Pasatiempo club dues to the Pacific Coast Women's Polo Association. She had paid most of the costs of the Pasatiempo field. She had paid for the initial grading and for installing the irrigation pipes. She had paid all maintenance costs. In 1935 alone, she had spent over $1,500 for maintenance and for additional irrigation supplies.[5]

The Pogonip Club Features Women's Polo

From the beginning, the purpose of the Pogonip Polo Club was the promotion of good polo on a good field. The new regulation grass field and the practice field were in such excellent condition that, early in 1936, Dorothy Wheeler set up a series of exhibition polo matches. She asked Eric Tyrrell-Martin, internationally famed polo player from England and manager at Del Monte, to bring a team to play; Dorothy joined them as one of the women players. Soon thereafter, Dorothy wrote a New York editor: "There are some of the English international team playing here, some of whom had seen a little of the women's polo in Europe, and they were most complimentary in saying that our California brand of women's polo was much faster and more open than any they had seen."[6]

This was just the start. Soon Pogonip would be a center for polo in the region, drawing players from all over to enjoy the fast turf of their fine new field. In mid October of 1936, eager to show off the field, the local men challenged the crack Del Monte team to a match. The Pogonip team was captained by Bob Law and included Bill Whitney, Tanner Wilson and Dorothy Wheeler. The Del Monte team, captained by Dick Collins, included Lester Stirling and a visitor, Winston Frost, captain of the Harvard team. Unfortunately, the local team was no match for Del Monte. Starting off badly, Pogonip ended up losing by an ignominious 8 to 2. Their consolation: the visitors were impressed with the new polo field and remarked that it "compared well with the best fields in the area."[7]

The Pogonip Polo Club was unique among polo clubs in California because it featured women's polo. Although men were encouraged to be members—and Dorothy Wheeler kept very busy enlisting new members—the emphasis was on women's polo. As Dorothy wrote her polo-playing friend Ann Jackson in Santa Barbara,

Two women polo players in a game at Pogonip; Ruth Cropp on the left, Barbara Worth riding up on the right. (Colleen McInerney-Meagher collection)

Dorothy and a team of young girls ready to play polo; from left Katherine Smith, Doreen Ashburnham, Dorothy Wheeler, Colleen McInerney, Wilma Kann with *Indy*, and Elaine McInerney. (Colleen McInerney-Meagher collection)

"The thing Deming and I have worked for for so long...is the development of a polo field and polo center where women, and not men, are given paramount consideration." She continued, "You have helped tremendously in this respect and women are not shunted off the field as they used to be, but in some places it is still difficult for them to get regular times to play."[8]

In another letter to Ann Jackson, Dorothy added more insight into her hopes for the new club, saying, "Possibly I am very foolish to underwrite even so small a Polo venture but as it is the only thing Deming and I really care about as we grow older we would like to see it develop...not necessarily for high-goal polo but for colt training, beginners, and fun."[9]

The Pasatiempo stables were no longer available to the Pogonip polo players. So Deming Wheeler built new stables for the Pogonip club to the left of the road leading up to the clubhouse. (These stables no longer exist, having been dismantled in December 1986.) The stables housed a "rent string" of polo ponies that were available to young riders and out-of-town visitors for a nominal fee.[10] Across the road from the stables, the Wheelers established a second polo field, the so-called "lower field" for practice games. The main field, the "upper field" was reserved for competitive games and tournaments.

Dorothy not only believed in encouraging women players. She also believed in encouraging all young people—boys as well as girls—who wanted to play polo. Many a budding polo player was grateful to the Wheelers for the loan of a well-trained polo pony. The club offered polo lessons to beginners. Young players learned "walk polo" on the lower grass field. Walk polo taught the basics of the various strokes and, most importantly, it taught the rules of the game. When a new player became proficient, she or he graduated to a gallop, then

pogonip

RIDING AND POLO STABLES

off Big Tree Highway

PHONE 1438-J

—

RATES
(As of June 1, 1937)

POLO:

Walk Polo	50c per period
Regular slow gallop polo for girls	$1.00 per period
Fast women's polo	1.25 per period
Fast gallop polo for men	1.50 per period
Anyone playing just one chukker	2.00 per period

REGULAR RIDING RATES:

First hour	$1.00
For an hour overtime	.50
Half day	2.50
All day	4.50
Group riding with escort	1.50
Breakfast rides	1.50
(Breakfast 50c additional)	
Moonlight rides	1.50
(Supper 50c additional)	

LESSONS:

Private lessons	12 for $15.00
Class lessons	12 for 12.00
Trail riding or ring polo	$1.00

Non-transferable ticket
$12 value for $10
May be used for any of the above

Fee schedule for polo classes at Pogonip in the summer of 1937. (Colleen McInerney-Meagher collection)

to some tournament play during the regular Saturday and Sunday games. Polo practice was held three times a week on the lower field.

Membership in the club was growing. Not only Santa Cruz provided members but polo players joined from all around California. By joining the Pogonip Polo Club they were eligible to play with the club in tournaments. Some early players to join were Ann and Pete Jackson of Santa Barbara, Barbara Worth of Sacramento, and Leone Hart, also of Sacramento.

In late November of 1936, Dorothy Wheeler's dream of playing high-goal women's polo in her own hometown came true. The Pogonip Polo Club was host to the four-day United States Women's Polo Association Circuit Championship. On the third day of the

The Champs! Shown here in front of the Pogonip clubhouse after winning the 1936 Northern Circuit Championship of the United States Women's Polo Association; from left, Barbara Worth, Leone Hart, Dorothy Wheeler, and Elaine McInerney. (Colleen McInerney-Meagher collection)

tournament, the Pogonip team defeated a team from Riviera to take home the Women's Association cup for the third year in a row. The Pogonip women's team went on to win the championship for seven years in a row.

The Men Play Too

Although devoted to women's polo, the Pogonip Polo Club did not neglect the men. Every Saturday and Sunday the club held informal games for mixed teams of both men and women. These games were played every week unless the women were playing in tournaments.

A number of local men played with the women in these games. Bob Law, one of the founders of the Pogonip Polo Club, enjoyed the polo at Pogonip. Haldane "Hank" Graham and his son Courtney "Corky" Graham, who started Plantronics in Santa Cruz in the 1960's, were two regular players. (Corky's mother, Adele, also played.) Bob Gillies and Bill Whitney, who trained the horses at Windy Hill, played at Pogonip. John Parker, a frequent player, was from Alameda, though his family owned a ranch in Santa Cruz.

Besides the local men, polo players such as Garret McEnerney and Bill Gilmore came from San Francisco to enjoy the good field and good times at Pogonip. An occasional player at Pogonip was Willie Tevis, Jr. He came from a wealthy California family and was known for establishing the 100-mile endurance ride, called the Tevis Cup, a ride that starts south of Truckee and ends one hundred miles west above the American River Canyon in the Gold Rush town of Auburn. Willie Tevis was memorable because he would fly his small plane in, land on the Pogonip polo field, play a few chukkers, and then fly off again.

There were, however, very few men-only games—perhaps only one or two over the years. A men's game might be scheduled if a team was visiting from out of town, but even then the local men usually had to borrow a woman player to fill out the team. There were just not enough men players, and besides the men enjoyed playing with the women, who almost always beat them if they played men against women!

A Sunday afternoon game at Pogonip in 1936 with a mixed team of men and women; four players in foreground from left: Marguerite Dellamonica, Elaine McInerney, Bill Gilmore, and Barbara Worth; an unknown man and Bob Law to the rear. The E. O. McCormick Estate, which later burned down, is in the left background. (Colleen McInerney-Meagher collection)

Chapter Seven

A Very Social Club

Pogonip Becomes a Social Center

Pogonip was not only about polo. By the fall of 1936, country club life at the Pogonip Polo Club was in full swing. The clubhouse was open for cocktails and dinner. On September 17, the club held a luncheon to celebrate the opening of their new swimming pool. The pool was thirty by sixty feet, tapering down to ten feet at the deep end. The luncheon was followed by an exhibition polo game; surely, the polo players and their guests cooled off in the new pool after the game.[1]

The first managers of the Pogonip Polo Club were Colonel and Mrs. Bing-Hall. The colonel and his lady had served their time in India and the dinner fare was redolent of the "Raj" with huge joints of beef (the English influence) and curries so hot Deming Wheeler wrapped his bald head in a towel while eating them (the Indian influence). A few years later Lucille McInerney became the hostess for Pogonip. In 1938, she had moved to Santa Cruz from Beverly Hills with her two polo-playing daughters Elaine and Colleen. She took up residence in the guesthouse at Windy Hill Farm and then took her first job as the hostess at Pogonip, a role she filled with charm and grace for a number of years.

The clubhouse was rustic. It had a rough exterior and used redwood saplings still covered with bark as a decorative scheme. The main reception room measured 25 by 40 feet with a huge stone fireplace in the center of the wall facing the entrance. On the left was a game room with ping-pong tables, a nickelodeon, and a life-size papier-mâché horse hiding the stairs to a balcony. The balcony had Pullman berths where visiting polo players could stay overnight. "Some say there are still players sealed up there."[2]

The swimming pool, which opened in September of 1936. Behind the pool is the building with the women's bathhouse. The room on the right with an entrance around the corner was known for many years as the "mouse house." The diving board was a gift from the cast of *Maid of Salem*, a movie made at Pogonip that September. (Colleen McInerney-Meagher collection)

To the right of the game room was a separate room with a bar and bar stools and several tables where the polo players and their guests would gather to replay the day's game. Black and white photos of polo players lined the walls. To the right of the main room was the dining room. A wall of windows at the front of the building looked out past the porch to the pool and beyond to the polo field.

In September of 1936, just as Pogonip was getting started, the producers of the movie *Maid of Salem* contracted to use the Pogonip polo field as the village green in their movie about Salem witch trials. Members of the company enjoyed the use of the club and, as a house gift, donated the diving board for the new pool. The rent for use of the polo field went to defray the cost of putting in the pool.[3]

Hollywood and Pogonip

Much has been made of the prevalence of Hollywood stars at Pogonip—very little of it accurate. Because of the popularity of polo in Hollywood, polo players came from Hollywood to play at the

Movies at Pogonip

Of the many movies made in Santa Cruz, three used the Pogonip Polo Club: *Maid of Salem* in 1936, *Stand up and Fight* in 1938 and, almost fifty years later in 1986, *The Lost Boys.*

Maid of Salem was directed by Frank Lloyd and distributed by Paramount Pictures; it starred Claudette Colbert and Fred MacMurray. Lloyd had already used Santa Cruz as a setting in 1935 when he brought the two frigates "Bounty" and "Pandora" to cast anchor off the Santa Cruz wharf and sent in a crew to film scenes for the highly acclaimed MGM movie, *Mutiny on the Bounty.*[4] A stickler for historical accuracy, Lloyd built an entire puritan village to represent Salem. The village was built on the William Colt ranch on Cave Gulch Road off Empire Grade in Santa Cruz. When the movie company left, the village was dismantled and the lumber left behind for local use.[5]

In November of 1938 MGM was once again in Santa Cruz, this time to make the movie *Stand Up and Fight*. The stars were Wallace Beery, Robert Taylor and Florence Rice. It was a western set in the nineteenth century and directed by Woody S. Van Dyke. It was an "excellent dual vehicle for veteran Beery and the up-and-coming Taylor."[6]

Central to the movie was a foxhunting episode, which required the ladies to ride sidesaddle dressed in long skirts and feathered hats. Two of the women who rode in the spectacle were on the Pogonip women's polo team. Barbara Worth was the double for Florence Rice and Elaine McInerney rode as an extra in several hunting scenes. Barbara, who was later elected to the Show Jumping Hall of Fame, wrote about her experience.

[continued next page]

Elaine McInerney riding sidesaddle as an extra in the movie *Stand Up and Fight*. (Colleen McInerney-Meagher collection)

"Not only was Miss Rice unable to ride a horse, she was extremely allergic to them."[7] Robert Taylor used a double also. According to Barbara one of the men, Bob "Red" Burns rode as a double for a woman as well as a man.

In one of the events Barbara was required to gallop across a creek and up a steep bank. Several riders had crossed before her and the incline had become very slippery. On the way up, Barbara's horse slid backwards into the water. "Fortunately for me, he twisted around so he fell into the water on his right side and not on his back. All I could think of was to clamp my right knee around the front horn and bind my left knee up against the leaping horn of that side saddle." She knew that her horse would get up and get her out of the water. "That situation proved rather conclusively that it is almost impossible to fall off of a side saddle unless one kicks one's legs free of the horns."[8]

Movie making was a profitable enterprise for Santa Cruz. The entire company took rooms at the Hotel Palomar while they were in town. In the nine days of shooting *Stand Up and Fight* in Santa Cruz, MGM spent over $30,000 for hotel accommodations, labor, supplies, and transportation.[9]

The Lost Boys was the third movie to use Pogonip as a setting. Significant scenes in *The Lost Boys* were filmed in the Pogonip clubhouse shortly before the clubhouse was condemned in 1987. (See Chapter Nine for a description of this movie.)

Barbara Worth's chair on the set of *Stand Up and Fight*; a polo player for Pogonip, she acted as double for star, Florence Rice. Standing behind the chair is an unidentified man and to the right, Colleen McInerney, another member of the Pogonip women's polo team, many of whom were extras in the movie.
(Photograph courtesy of William H. Oakford, Barbara Worth's husband.)

club, but none of them were stars. For example, Louise Tracy, Spencer Tracy's wife, and their son John, were frequent visitors, but Spencer himself never came to Pogonip. He was, like many other Hollywood celebrities, an occasional guest of Marion Hollins at Pasatiempo.

Pasatiempo was where the stars visited when they came to Santa Cruz. Marion Hollins had many friends in the movie business and was a gracious hostess to them all. Not only Spencer Tracy and his wife Louise stayed with her when they were in town; she also entertained Walt Disney and Will Rogers. She was particularly attached to Mary Pickford and her husband Buddy Rogers, and she entertained these friends lavishly and frequently. When Claudette Colbert came to Santa Cruz to star in *Maid of Salem*, she and her maid were Marion's guests at Pasatiempo.[10]

According to Dorothy Wheeler, Mrs. Spencer Tracy, Mary Pickford and Richard Barthelmess were "frequent" visitors at Pogonip.[11] Elaine McInerney amended this statement. She said that Mary Pickford, Buddy Rogers, and Carol Landis were guests of Marion Hollins, who on at least one occasion brought them to Pogonip for the day. Richard Barthelmess came to Pogonip to watch his daughter Mary play polo when she played there as a member of the Douglas School team. One year Victor McLaughlin's wife came over for a hunter trial—and entered and won the hunter event.[12]

A Full Gamut of Activities

The Pogonip Polo Club was from its inception the scene of many festive dinners and drinks at the bar. It would get particularly lively on Sunday nights after the weekend polo games. The players gathered around the bar to replay the day's events, and Frank Wilson, with his guitar, led barbershop quartets.

The club was the setting for lunches and suppers and dances for a "congenial group." The group was kept congenial by restricting membership to those people who satisfied a membership committee "whose names are to be kept secret to the membership at large, so that no difficulties can develop if some names are not included."[13] This was typical of private clubs of that era—as well as of some private clubs to this day.

Pogonip charged its members annual dues depending on the type of membership. In 1936, the club offered three types of membership:

1. Clubhouse or social membership dues were $50 and allowed family use of the club for all privileges except polo.

2. Playing membership dues for adults were $75 and allowed all family privileges, plus two polo players.

3. Playing fee for junior polo players was $10 and offered no privileges except polo.

A nine-member Board of Directors determined the club rules and the penalties for rule infractions. They decided on admission fees and dues, and approved the nomination and election of new members.

The stated purpose of the club was to "promote equestrian and other outdoor sports and social intercourse among its members."[14] It was a non-profit organization. Some of the many events at the new club were gymkhanas for the children, hunter trials for the adults, fashion shows for the young women, the Pogonip Bluerock and Skeet Club for the sharpshooters among the men, and almost always a Bridge game was going on.

left: Patch of the Pogonip Bluerock and Skeet Club given to David L. Wilson for "50 straight." (Courtesy of Tanner G. Wilson) below: Member of the Bluerock and Skeet Club shooting at Pogonip. (Museum of Art & History)

Gymkhanas

The Junior Gymkhana and Horse Show, an event for young members, was first held in the fall of 1937. It continued as a yearly event until the last was held in August of 1941. Essentially, a gymkhana is a set of games played on horseback. The games might include a potato race, musical chairs, or an egg and spoon race.

Events such as the potato race or pie eating contest or musical chairs were surely the most fun for the young contestants. Musical chairs was played just as it is played in any kindergarten except on horseback: the rider jumped off his or her horse when the music stopped, raced to the nearest chair, sat in the chair until the music started up, jumped back on the horse, and continued until a rider claimed the last chair to win. In a pie-eating contest, the aim was to jump off your horse, eat all the pie on a plate with your fingers, remount and ride to the finish line.

A Pogonip gymkhana invariably started with a grand parade in which both riders and horses were rated for the best English outfit and the best Western outfit. The gymkhana also included horse show events, where English riders were judged on Seat and Hands, and

Pat Pagen in a pie-eating contest at Pogonip in 1940.
(Colleen McInerney-Meagher collection)

Program of Events

PRIZES AND RIBBONS

GRAND PARADE
Best Western Outfit   —   Best English Outfit
Trophy donated by   Trophy donated by
Mr. and Mrs. Bruce Sharpe   Mrs. John L. Pagen
*To be judged on the basis of 75% for riders outfit
and 25% for the horse*
1st, 2nd, and 3rd Ribbons

POTATO RACE
Trophy donated by, The Frank Wilson Family
1st, 2nd, and 3rd Ribbons

SEATS AND HANDS CLASS
Trophy donated by, Mr. Carleton White
For English Riders Only
Riders to perform at a walk, trot, canter etc., as desired by judges
1st, 2nd, and 3rd Ribbons

STOCK HORSE CLASS
To be judged on the performance of the horse and rider
Trophy donated by, Mr and Mrs. Stanford Smith
1st, 2nd, and 3rd Ribbons

TEAMS OF 4 RELAY RACE
Advance Riders
Trophies donated by
Pogonip Stables   —   Miss Doreen Ashburnham
Mr. C. S. Henry   —   Mr. and Mrs. Paul Case
1st, 2nd, and 3rd Ribbons

PIE EATING CONTEST
Trophy donated by, Mrs. Alfred Phillips
1st, 2nd, and 3rd Ribbons

HACKAMORE CLASS
To be judged on the performance of the horse and rider
Trophy donated by, Mr. Deming Wheeler
1st, 2nd, and 3rd Ribbons

TROTTING RACE
Trophy donated by, Mr. and Mrs. John Parker
1st, 2nd, and 3rd Ribbons

POLO PONY CLASS
Trophy donated by, Mrs. Deming Wheeler
1st, 2nd, and 3rd Ribbons

OLD CLOTHES RACE
Trophy donated by, Mrs. Luther Dunlap
1st, 2nd, and 3rd Ribbons

BALLOON BATTLE
Trophy donated by, Mrs. Donald Gregory
1st, 2nd, and 3rd Ribbons

MUSICAL CHAIRS
Trophy donated by, Mrs. Boudinot Conner
1st, 2nd, and 3rd Ribbons

GYMKHANA AND HORSESHOW
COMMITTEE

Miss Jane Phillips
Miss Barbara Sharpe
Miss Elaine McInerney
Mr. John Parker, Jr.
Mr. Richard Parker
Mr. Corky Graham

JUDGES
Mr. Clifford Kilfoyl
Mr. Eric Tyrrell-Martin
Capt. James M. Palmer

MASTER OF CEREMONIES
Dr. John T. Harrington
Mr. William Hyde Irwin

TIME AND SCOREKEEPER
Mrs. Lucille McInerney
Miss Pat Phillips
Miss Barbara Sharpe

Program of Events for a Junior Gymkhana and Horse Show at Pogonip in 1940.
(Colleen McInerney-Meagher collection)

Western riders were judged in Stock Horse and Hackamore classes. Youngsters, aged five to twelve years, could enter a trotting race.

Hunter Trials

Starting in 1939 and continuing through 1942, hunter trials were a yearly event at Pogonip. Each year, Pogonip joined Pebble Beach in putting on a weekend show with both a steeplechase and a hunter trial. Pebble Beach hosted the pair of events on the first day of the weekend and Pogonip hosted them the following day. Pogonip boasted an outstanding hunter trial course designed by Barbara Worth, Dick Collins, and a Major Calbent.

In a steeplechase, the riders race together on a flat area over hurdles made of timber or brush. The Pogonip steeplechase was run

Illustration of the various pitfalls encountered on the hunter trial course at Pogonip, by Bill Irwin (Colleen McInerney-Meagher collection)

Unidentified woman riding in the hunter event at Pogonip. (Colleen McInerney-Meagher collection)

on the upper polo field over portable hurdles. In a hunter trial, individual riders follow a rough cross-country course up hill and down dale, over fences and other barriers in a race against the clock.

Hunter trials originated in Ireland. As described in a *Sentinel* article, "The Trials really started when Irish horse dealers would send the horses over a course in front of prospective buyers in an effort to convince the boys with the money-bags that their horses were what they wanted. The horse that was the better jumper usually attracted the better price and the riders would spare nothing to convince the purchasers. Tough obstacles were placed in front of the horses but they usually managed to give a good account of themselves."[15]

The race at Pogonip covered a mile and a half of rolling hills, deep gulleys and level country. There were a number of hazards and it was not an event for novice riders. There were jumps over logs and other hazardous objects; one jump was over a chicken coop; at another place the rider had to open and close a gate. One gallop was down the side of a steep gulley. There were two judges: one to observe the horses and pick his favorite, the other to rate the horses on their faults, which included run outs, disobedience, and refusals. Faults were counted against the horse's time in the race.

The hunter trials and steeplechase at Pogonip were popular not only locally, but also with participants from all around the state. At one event Dorothy Wheeler defeated Willie Tevis, Jr. in the steeplechase, and Mrs. Victor McLaughlin won the hunter trial.[16]

Bicycle polo on the polo field in front of the clubhouse, circa 1937. Note the short mallet. Bill Whitney on the left, Tanner Wilson in foreground, and Elaine McInerney in helmet. (Colleen McInerney-Meagher collection)

Other Activities

Bicycle polo was played mostly by young men and women members as an amusing alternative to horse polo. The players used the same short mallets that beginners used for walk polo.

The young women members of Pogonip enjoyed a tradition of summer fashion shows. The theme was frequently tropical—hints of the Hawaiian Islands in leis and ukuleles. The fashion shows, like many other Pogonip events, were fundraisers.

A fashion show with a Hawaiian theme at Pogonip circa 1940, featuring local and visiting belles.
(Colleen McInerney-Meagher collection)

Chapter Eight

Pogonip At War

World War II Comes to Santa Cruz

On a beautiful sunny Sunday in December 1941, some young polo players were driving to Pogonip to play when they heard on the radio that the Japanese had attacked Pearl Harbor. One of these players, Colleen McInerney, recalls that moment: "Being all of 15 years old and living in the small coastal town of Santa Cruz, California, I hadn't the faintest idea where Pearl Harbor was. Little did I realize at that moment that soon the whole world would change and my childhood would be gone forever." Shortly thereafter the young men would go off to war. One of these men was Colleen's future fiancé, John Parker. Another was her sister Elaine's husband, Lowell Bready, who had been news editor of the *Santa Cruz Sentinel*.

Polo continued at Pogonip, but in a dramatically different way. Tournament polo ceased altogether. The United States Women's Polo Association stopped meeting and playing, never to resume. The Pogonip women's team dispersed and the few women who remained played on the weekends with any available men. Into this hiatus rode Dorothy Wheeler with a bold plan to enlist the Pogonip women polo players in the war effort.

The Women's Mounted Corps

With the U. S. entry into the war, Dorothy Deming Wheeler immediately began to think of ways she could help. Her biggest contribution was to make the United States Women's Polo Association available to the American Red Cross as an auxiliary to the Red Cross Motor Corps. A Mounted Corps would provide

Two members of the Mounted Corps lead a horse carrying a Stokes stretcher and other supplies. One of the admirable innovations of the corps was their use of this stretcher—a long metal basket that kept wounded victims from moving or slipping. By carrying the stretcher on horseback, they greatly increased the safety with which an injured person could be brought out of rough country. (*United States Women's Polo Association Manual of Field Training and Maneuvers*, Colleen McInerney-Meagher collection)

services similar to the Motor Corps but in rural and mountainous areas where cars did not have access. She planned to help with preparedness and disaster relief programs and to make her mounted corps available to the county Civil Defense authorities.[1]

In the early days of the war, Dorothy imagined stranded pilots shot down in the backcountry whom she, with her trained horsewomen, would rescue. As she described it, the Mounted Corps would be "trained to deliver messages, to transport the injured, destroy incendiary bombs, and signal for aid in all emergencies."[2]

Dorothy Wheeler traveled to Washington to present her plans and by June 1942, the United States Red Cross had welcomed her into their fold.[3] Soon she had a uniform and was recruiting the young women polo players to join her. Their official title was the Women's Mounted Unit of the Red Cross Motor Corps. Dorothy, however, always referred to them as the United States Women's Polo Association Mounted Corps Auxiliary to the Red Cross.

The members of the corps were required to take a Red Cross first aid class. The volunteer group wore long-sleeved dark green shirts with an emblem on the left sleeve to identify the corps. They had to learn to strap the Stokes stretcher (a wire body basket used by firefighters) onto a horse to rescue the men. So successful were the techniques of the Mounted Corps that Army experts became interested, and considered adopting the Mounted Corps' horseback rescue methods.

Dorothy Wheeler wrote a manual for the Mounted Corps: *The United States Women's Polo Association Manual of Field Training and Maneuvers*. The training included learning to recognize military insignia, learning to read maps of the county, to find fire trails, and to read a compass. In addition, the women learned how to deliver messages and supplies to firefighters, ride cross-country, pack an extra horse with supplies, ride at night, and set up camp.[4]

The patch Dorothy Wheeler designed for the uniforms of her Mounted Corps. Notice she does not include the Red Cross name in this design, but shows two crossed polo mallets and a horseshoe within the name, "U.S. Women's Polo Assoc. Mounted Corps."
(Pat Horton Scrapbook)

The travois was another method for transporting the wounded that Dorothy Wheeler experimented with. This photograph was taken on the Pogonip polo field. Pat Horton on the horse, Dorothy Wheeler with hand on hip, and Adele Graham opposite with her hand on the travois. All are wearing variations on the mounted corps uniform. (Colleen McInerney-Meagher collection)

The troops traveled to Tevis ranch in Marin County where Willie Tevis, Jr. was their host. There, they performed maneuvers and met other members of the corps from San Mateo, San Francisco, Livermore, and Berkeley. At that time some sixty women belonged to the USWPA Mounted Corps.

At least two other communities joined with Dorothy in trying to establish a Mounted Corps. The St. Helena (California) Relief Committee proposed in May of 1942 that they form a mounted corps that would, like the Santa Cruz corps, be used for mounted defense and rescue work.[5] Subsequently, San Francisco was to form a Mounted Unit of the Red Cross under the direction of Mrs. Walter Heller.[6]

Full of ideas about how to help the war effort, Dorothy Wheeler campaigned to have parking lots where riders could "park" their horses in downtown Santa Cruz. With car rationing certain and bicycles possibly becoming scarce, she wrote, "I foresee the day when many fine saddle horses will be used for transportation. Why not anticipate the problem and establish such a parking lot now?"[7] And

Santa Cruz responded. A horse parking lot was established at 27 Front Street with a watering trough and several hitching racks. For a small recompense, a neighbor, Vincent Bertorelli, would take time from his vegetable patch to watch the lot. As with the Mounted Corps, Dorothy's idea for a horse parking lot received national attention. Other communities were receptive to her idea.[8]

Navy Relief Polo Exhibition in Golden Gate Park

Even before they were official, the women's Mounted Corps strutted their stuff as part of an extraordinary demonstration of horsemanship put on in Golden Gate Park to raise money for Navy Relief. On Sunday, May 3, 1942, the women of the Pogonip Polo Club were invited to play an exhibition game against the Riviera team, Tierra del Rey, as part of the Navy Relief Exhibition. They played a fast match that ended in a 2 to 2 tie.

The polo game was not the only event to take place that day at the polo field in San Francisco's Golden Gate Park. More than 300 horses entertained the 8,000 people in attendance. A grand parade included palominos, pintos, thoroughbreds, polo ponies, and cow ponies. The First California Cavalry, the mounted police, the militia, and the Pogonip Women's Mounted Corps—in their first public

Dorothy Wheeler (in dark shirt) tries to hook the mallet that Dorothy Rodgers is using to hit a forward shot in the Navy Relief game at Golden Gate Park, May 3, 1942. (Photo by Frank Gordon; Colleen McInerney-Meagher collection)

appearance—all took part in the grand parade.

Shortly after their appearance in the parade for Navy Relief at Golden Gate Park, the Mounted Corps was invited back to San Francisco. This time they were to take part in the celebration of MacArthur Day at Kezar Stadium in June of 1942.

The event, as described in a San Francisco paper, was very grand and very patriotic. The band played China's national anthem, Britain's *God Save The King*, Russia's *Internationale*, and finally the *Star Spangled Banner*. (It is ironic to be reminded that all three of these countries, China and Russia as well as Britain, were WWII allies of the United States.) Then, "in perfect timing, just as the Stars and Stripes were flung to the breeze from the tallest flagstaff of all, squadron after squadron of blitz-fast American interceptor planes— P38s and the wicked P40's came howling out of the eastern sky to dive and sweep in ear splitting thunder across the field, so low that you could see every detail of these craft which are standing by, day and night, to guard San Francisco against the threat of enemy raiders."[9]

The arena held 35,000 people, and the Pogonip Women's Mounted Corp proudly galloped their horses into the stadium carrying the American flag.

Argentineans Play Polo at Pogonip

In August of 1942, three Argentine polo players, Fernando Mihanovich, George Small, and Ramon Bigorie, arrived at Pogonip. They came from Buenos Aires where they owned ranches and polo ponies and where they were first-rate players. While visiting in San Francisco they had heard about the polo club in Santa Cruz. Most of the men players in Santa Cruz had gone off to war, but the Pogonip women players were still able to play along with the few local men.

The Argentineans, who were not combatants in World War II, decided to stay for the entire summer and play in the mixed games held on the weekends. The Argentineans were noted world wide for their polo playing, but even more they were envied for the quality of their polo ponies. They were accustomed to much better horses than the Pogonip stable ponies—which were not the superior thoroughbreds raised at Windy Hill.

Despite the quality of the ponies available to them, they were good sports. Every weekend that summer, the Argentine visitors

"A Bit Of The Nip." Argentine polo players pop a cork after a match in the summer of 1942; from left: the Argentine consul, Roberto Lainez; Paul Case; Fernando Mihanovich pouring the bubbly; George Small; Pat Horton; and Colleen McInerney with *Sleepy*. (Colleen McInerney-Meagher collection)

joined in tournaments between teams of two men and two women. There were trophies for the winners and occasionally the teams would pop a bottle of champagne and drink from the winning vessels.

Polo Players Boost Navy Morale

The Argentineans were not the only visitors to play polo at Pogonip during World War II. The 107th Cavalry also came to play. In 1942 they were stationed at Fort Ord in Monterey and a Lieutenant Undercoffer was their commanding officer. The young women of the Pogonip Club gave him the nickname, "Lieut."

In addition to polo games, Dorothy Wheeler put on formal dances for the men of the 107th Cavalry and, as usual, conscripted her young women polo players. They were to do their bit for the war effort by dancing with the men as well as playing polo with them.

Dorothy Wheeler and her Women's Mounted Corps with the sailors and marines from the U.S. Naval hospital in Santa Cruz, setting out from the Pogonip stables for a picnic. (Photo by Harley Lewis; Colleen McInerney-Meagher collection)

After a picnic lunch, the sailors and marines sing around the campfire with the young women of the Mounted Corps. Pat Barker is on guitar, and Dorothy Wheeler is in the background. (Photo by Harley Lewis; Colleen McInerney-Meagher collection)

In 1944 the U.S. Naval Hospital at the Casa del Rey Hotel was home to sailors and Marines recuperating from combat fatigue, sickness and wounds. To boost their morale, Dorothy Wheeler organized picnics for any convalescents well enough to ride a horse. Twice a week they set out on horseback into the countryside. Dorothy provided mounts from the Pogonip stables and the young women of her Mounted Corps acted as guides.[10]

They would carry a supply of provisions into the mountains where they would have a picnic lunch cooked in the open. Then they would sing around the campfire. As a national magazine wrote, "a pretty girl, a guitar, and the old songs of the range sung under the open sky" is a tonic that's hard to beat. The hospital officials reported that the horseback trips gave a powerful boost to the men's morale and sped their recovery.[11]

Plane Crash at Pogonip

The Women's Mounted Corps may not have had a chance to rescue downed fliers in the mountains and back country of Santa Cruz County, but Dorothy Wheeler was able to rescue one downed flier right in her own back yard. On an April day in 1944, Lieutenant John R. Philips crashed his plane, an Army P-39 or Airacobra, into a palm tree near the Pogonip clubhouse.

His plane came in low and almost took the roof off the clubhouse before plowing a deep furrow for 50 feet or so in the earth. The plane crashed through a fence and was whirled around when its left wing caught on the palm tree.

This was Dorothy's chance. She seized her kit and was first on the scene in "nothing flat." She telephoned the local police station and then gave the dazed pilot first aid and removed him to the clubhouse. Soon sirens were wailing, as the police, an ambulance, a fire truck, and the navy shore patrol sped to the scene. The plane was badly wrecked. The engine was thrown a hundred feet away, the cockpit torn open, and both wings ruined. Luckily, the plane did not catch fire and the pilot was thrown clear. He suffered only a bump on the head and "a lot of butterflies in his stomach." The pilot was last seen sitting on a wing of his plane, writing a report.[12]

Chapter Nine

Pogonip Carries On

Polo Fades Away

Throughout the Second World War, the Pogonip Polo Club remained open and some of the women continued to play polo with the few men who had not left for the service. After the war ended, some people still played polo at Pogonip. But there was no organized women's polo and there were no tournaments—the United States Women's Polo Association had effectively ceased to exist.

Pogonip continued to host polo games through the spring and summer of 1947.[1] One of the last games at Pogonip was played on July 6, 1947. A local Pogonip team played a combined team from Stockton and Sacramento. The local foursome included Dr. Frederick Barron, Dick Collins, Pat Horton Winnett and Elaine McInerney-Kozak. Only two of the players on the opposing team were named: Dr. Neil Johnson and Dr. Clapper. The Pogonip team won 12 to 2.[2]

One of the more exciting moments occurred before the game when Dr. Johnson tried to land his plane on the Pogonip field. An unexpected wind caused him to make six tries before he succeeded in getting his light plane onto the ground. This reminded the local spectators of the crash that had occurred in 1944.[3]

In May of 1948, Pogonip hosted the Spring Invitational Steeplechase at which one last polo game was played between Pogonip and San Mateo. The festive day included horse races for the children and a "Ladies race" as well as the traditional steeplechase over the British-style course that Pogonip had laid out.[4] There were no more polo games after 1948. Right after the steeplechase, Pogonip briefly shut its doors. It was time for renovation and to rethink the role of the club.

After closing down for renovation, Pogonip reopened in June

1948 as a private social club. The club celebrated its reopening with a "Welcome Home Dorothy" dinner dance attended by 150 people. Dorothy Wheeler, who would be the first president of the new club, had just returned from a long trip.[5] She was succeeded as president in 1950 by Sidney Carter and in 1951 by Tanner Wilson.[6]

The Wheelers Step Down

The decline of polo at Pogonip coincided with the Wheelers no longer being a powerful force in the governance of the club. Deming Wheeler had been in poor health for some time, and in the early morning of March 31, 1946, he died of a heart attack at his home at Windy Hill Farm. Dorothy took his body to Terre Haute, Indiana, where it was buried in the family plot.[7] She carried on, but her life no longer centered on polo and Pogonip.

Dorothy was still in excellent health. She continued to be interested in Pogonip, but she was building a new life elsewhere. She took an apartment in San Francisco. She took trips. In her scrapbooks are pictures of her happily dancing on a cruise ship. In 1948 she took a two and a half months-long tour of South America where she visited with polo players.[8]

Then, on September 24, 1949, she remarried. Her husband, Edgar Forbes Wilson, was a San Francisco attorney, a sports fan, and an opera buff. After a brief weekend wedding trip to Northern California, the bride and groom were "at home" at Windy Hill Farm. Thereafter the couple made their home in San Francisco and spent weekends at Windy Hill.[9] On her weekends in Santa Cruz, Dorothy seldom missed a Sunday night dinner at the club. She continued to entertain each member of the Pogonip Club at least once a year at her Windy Hill home. It became a

Dorothy Wheeler Wilson at her 79th birthday bash at Pogonip in 1974.
(*Santa Cruz Sentinel*)

tradition to hold a big birthday bash for her at Pogonip every year on or near her January 23rd birthday.[10]

From the early 1960s thru January of 1975, the club held the traditional "Dorothy's Birthday Party." On her 79th birthday in 1974, Pogonip's "Grande Dame" was honored by 85 members and their guests.[11] The next year, the last year of her life, she confided to friends that she wanted to make it to her eightieth birthday party, and according to her old friend, Bill Irwin, "she was there, alert and lucid after a period of being confined to bed. Many friends from the past, sensing that it was the last, attended the January party."[12]

Dorothy Deming Wheeler Wilson died on March 22, 1975.[13] Her husband, Edgar Forbes Wilson, had preceded her in death on July 10, 1970.

Pogonip Becomes a Social Club

Now that it was no longer a polo club, the Pogonip Club was primarily social. It held frequent lunches for its members, occasional dinners, and lots of bridge games. Special parties could be arranged as well as weddings. The swimming pool was available and there was always ping-pong in the game room.

Tennis eventually replaced polo as the club sport. In a letter to the Cowell trustees (undated, but probably November 1973), the president of Pogonip asked the Cowell Foundation for the assurance of a five-year lease so they could go ahead and raise money for tennis

Annual mixed doubles tournament, Pogonip, September 1977. Joel Marini serves to Frank Gonzales and Mary Haber. (Museum of Art & History)

Sidebar

The Club Name

After Pogonip reopened as a social club, the newspapers could not seem to agree on its name. Some still called it the "Pogonip Polo Club," others the "Pogonip Country Club," and still others called it simply the "Pogonip Club." For instance, in June of 1948, the *Sentinel* reported that the Pogonip Country Club held a dinner dance to celebrate its reopening. A 1951 article announcing a new president called it the Pogonip Polo Club, while similar articles in 1952 and 1955 call it respectively, the Pogonip Club and the Pogonip Country Club.[14]

The club itself seemed equally indecisive, sometimes calling itself the Pogonip Polo Club and sometimes the Pogonip Club. A number of official documents and some official stationary kept the old name, perhaps to honor the club's long history. In 1986, the club briefly considered having two clubs with slightly different agendas: one the Pogonip Club and the other the Pogonip Polo Club. This idea did not take hold.

Then, in August of 1989, the board addressed the issue directly and amended the bylaws of the club to declare the official name to be the "Pogonip Club." Yet the minutes of the board meeting still referred to the Pogonip Polo Club. At this time and on into the 1990s, the club stationery and official documents kept the word Polo and images of polo players in its logo.[15]

Mostly however, members simply referred to their beloved club as "Pogonip."

courts.[16] The Sentinel reported "younger members are taking a more active interest in Pogonip Club, with the building of two tennis courts."[17] By the summer of 1974, the two tennis courts were built and tennis was in full swing. Annual tournaments were held every year in late summer with trophies for the winners.

From the 1950s through the 1980s Pogonip remained a small private social club where friends met to eat lunch, swim, play tennis or play cards. The club held regularly scheduled luncheon and dinner

Birthday party for
Olivia Suchman
(back to camera),
April 1985.
(Museum of Art &
History)

parties. They celebrated all holidays. On Thanksgiving for a few years
in the 1960s, Pogonip's gracious Yugoslavian manager, Miho "Mike"
Birimisia, provided a turkey dinner for any member-families who
chose to attend. Each family had their own turkey at their own table
and, best of all, could take home the leftovers.[18]

Christmas was another day for festivities with tree-trimming
suppers and celebratory luncheons. New Year's Eve also provided
an excuse for a party. At Easter, there was usually a brunch and an
Easter Egg hunt. Depending on when it fell, Easter could be the
occasion for opening the pool. Members held their birthday parties

Clubhouse
interior
decorated
for
Christmas
ladies'
luncheon,
December
1985.
(Museum of
Art & History)

A horse-drawn carriage brings a wedding couple up the drive to Pogonip, April, 1985.
(Museum of Art & History)

at the club and also held parties for their children.

For a number of years, non-members could come up to enjoy lunch between 12 noon and two on Tuesday through Saturday and for Sunday brunch between eleven and two. Only members, however, could use the pool and tennis courts. The club also made itself available for weddings. Many Santa Cruz couples were married at Pogonip; some were members, some not. The weddings were frequently held outdoors so guests could enjoy the panoramic view of the ocean.

In 1984, Pogonip could pride itself on being the "oldest continuously operating private club in the county."[19] The next few years showed the effects of good management. By 1986, the club was making a profit. The grounds and clubhouse were still in need of maintenance, but the money to make the repairs was coming in.

In the summer of 1986, Pogonip looked forward to a surprising source of funds. They planned to lease their beloved, but funky, clubhouse to Warner Brothers as a movie set. The money would come in handy. The Board of Directors made a long list of capital improvements and they looked forward to retiring an outstanding bank loan.[20]

Clubhouse Setting In Vampire Film

The Pogonip Club negotiated a lease with Warner Brothers that would give them $30,000 for using the clubhouse from May 12 through June 13, 1986 for setup, shooting, and striking the set. If the actual shooting closed the clubhouse for more than six days, Warner Brothers would pay Pogonip an additional $1,500 per day. The club retained use of its premises for two scheduled events, a barbeque on

Film poster showing the lights of the Santa Cruz boardwalk. The three stars are Jami Gertz, Kiefer Sutherland, and Jason Patric. (www.katy berry.com)

above: New entrance to the clubhouse with rustic gate created for the *The Lost Boys* set. left: New paths, fences, trees, and benches changed the exterior of the Pogonip clubhouse. (Museum of Art & History)

May 28 and a wedding on June 14. As part of the contract, Warner Brothers donated two cases of champagne for the wedding.[21]

In June of 1986, director Joel Shumacher came to Santa Cruz to make his spoof on vampire films. Called "easily one of the smartest and funniest vampire movies ever made," it was set in the mythical seaside town of Santa Carla, a thinly veiled Santa Cruz complete with boardwalk and coastal caves.[22]

The clubhouse at Pogonip was the set for Grandpa's house and it looked every bit the home of an eccentric loner—dark and ramshackle. Nevertheless, the *The Lost Boys* crew made many superficial changes to the relatively sedate clubhouse to turn it into a horror-movie set. Most of the changes were to the exterior.

They built an entirely new entrance to the clubhouse that featured a large rustic gate with a carved wooden owl at its apex. The swimming pool was not appropriate to the movie, so the crew covered it with a tarpaulin and laid shrubs on top to make it look like wild scrubland. They mounted antlers and elk hides on the clubhouse walls. They made (or found) large wooden carvings, stuffed animals, and rough found-object sculptures, which they placed here and there in and around the clubhouse. They made a new artificial path leading up to the clubhouse delineated by rocks and picket fences. And they installed a wilderness of trees which, though set in planters, appeared to be part of the natural landscape.

The movie raised hackles locally when a *San Jose Mercury- News* headline proclaimed, "A city's reputation at stake—teen vampire film raises specter of Santa Cruz' past." In the accompanying article, Film critic Glenn Lovell dwelled on the film's reference to "Santa Carla" as "the murder capital of the world."[23] Local officials and the people associated with the film at the local level laughed off the notion that filmgoers would associate its comic horrors with Santa Cruz. A Warner Brothers production assistant explained that the reference to the "murder capital of the world" was part of the script long before Santa Cruz was chosen as the film's site.[24]

Several thousand local residents turned out to work as extras, playing a variety of roles: family types, street people, punks, surfers, roller skaters, and hippies. At the time, *The Lost Boys* was the largest film production to come to the area.[25] It would not, however, be the last. Many more films would be made in the city, but no more were made at Pogonip.

Pogonip Golden Anniversary Dinner
Saturday, November 15, 1986

Menu

Complimentary hors d'oeuvres, oyster bar
and champagne
7 - 8

Prime ribs with horseradish

Oven baked potatoes

Mixed vegetable medly

Romaine, parmesan, walnut and heart
of palm salad

Chocolate decadence

Coffee and tea

Live music, jazz & swing quartet 7:30-12
25. per person

Commemorative T-shirts will
be available for purchase
from the bar.   Seating limited
to 150!

Menu for the 50ᵗʰ Anniversary Dinner at Pogonip. (Colleen McInerney-Meagher collection)

Fiftieth Anniversary of The Pogonip Polo Club

October of 1986 marked the 50th anniversary of the founding of the Pogonip Polo Club. In keeping with its very social traditions, a party was planned for the occasion. On November 15, 1986, past and present members of the club joined to celebrate this anniversary with a festive dinner.

As part of the celebration, the club put up a display honoring its history. Dorothy Deming Wheeler had left three large scrapbooks to Special Collections at the University of California at Santa Cruz. Forty-four photographs from that collection, showing the women polo players from the glory days of the 1930s and 40s, were mounted on the dining room walls. Elaine McInerney-Kozak, arranged an exhibition of her numerous silver polo trophies in a glass case. The television set in the playroom showed the 1940 newsreel of a polo match played between the girls of the Douglas School team and a Pogonip women's team.[26] But 1986 was probably the last year of the club's halcyon days. Early in 1987, the Pogonip Club faced a problem that would challenge its very existence.[27]

Clubhouse Condemned

"The clubhouse, with its bowing timbers and dusty stone fireplace, sits bedraggled but defiant, like an aging debutant in need of a makeover."[28] Undoubtedly it was this decaying aspect of the clubhouse that had led Warner Brothers to choose it as a set for *The*

Lost Boys. Just a few months later, before the club had a chance to use the movie money to spruce up its building and grounds, the clubhouse was condemned for further use.

On February 10, 1987 the county building inspector, Lou Bacigalupi, posted a warning on the clubhouse that the building was unsafe for occupation. He reported that: "The roof is in real dire straits. One wall is leaning at a 6- to 10-degree angle. Four-by-four rafters are severely bowed. The tongue-and-groove roofing is beginning to separate from each other."

The owners of the property, the S. H. Cowell Foundation, had alerted the county to the state of the building. Cowell was currently spending about $40,000 a year to maintain the 614-acre property and patrol its diverse acres. (The Pogonip Club leased only the clubhouse and about two and a half acres of surrounding land.) Cowell had hired an engineering firm to inspect the clubhouse. After receiving the engineer's report, Bacigalupi said he "had no option except to go up there."

Bacigalupi further acknowledged that, although there had been no complaints about its condition, the clubhouse had probably been unsafe for many years. He said that when the Planning Department held a party there a few years before, he felt unsafe dancing on the clubhouse floor. Nevertheless, he had never gone up to inspect it; in his official capacity he was not aware that the clubhouse was unsafe.

The two caretakers who were living at the clubhouse had to move. The restaurant, which had been housed in the clubhouse, was closed.[29] The incomparable view of the city and Monterey Bay remained, but there was little else. In the summer the club served drinks to members from the caretaker's hut. The pool still worked but because of problems with the antique water line, there were no showers. Still, the loyal members continued to frequent the club, playing tennis on the courts and bringing their children to play in the pool. By 1989, according to the caretaker, Jim Ellis, "What the club really boils down to are the two tennis courts."[30]

The Last Years

As it turned out, the summer of 1986 was the last summer that members could enjoy their clubhouse. Nevertheless, the club kept going for almost seven years. The devotion of its members was remarkable. Without a clubhouse and with declining membership, the Pogonip Club still managed to be a magical place.

In later years, members would recall lazy days at Pogonip. "We go with the kids on those Saturday and Sunday afternoons when it gets to be three o'clock and you're wondering what to do. They would play tennis and swim and we'd sit around and talk to friends. It's been a whole way of life that has existed in Santa Cruz for decades."[31] The club was a place to relax and enjoy the beauties of a leisurely life. As an early member claimed, "It's peaceful and beautiful up there on the hill." Pogonip was a "place where you can get away from the rush and mad dash of the world today."[32]

Tables set up by the poolside at the Pogonip Club in 1988. Without the clubhouse, snacks were served from the caretaker's hut. (Dan Coyro)

Chapter Ten

Sycamore Grove Camp

At the same time that Santa Cruz society was going up the hill to play golf and, later, polo on the main Pogonip property, another simpler resort was thriving down below in the area once called Sycamore Flat. Between 1921 and the early 1960s, Sycamore Grove Camp flourished on the banks of the San Lorenzo River.

Sycamore Grove Camp was an auto camp catering mainly to families from out of town. Over the years "thousands of people from all over the world" came to camp in tents or cabins at this shady spot by the river. They came by car, often year after year to the same campsite or cabin. Primarily a summer resort, families also came in the winter for holidays and special occasions. Even a group of gypsies came regularly for a number of years. People from Santa Cruz also came, as Sycamore Grove was the best spot in town to swim in the San Lorenzo River.[1]

The entrance to the camp was off Big Trees Road (what is now Highway 9), half a mile north of the Golf Club Road entrance to Pogonip. This area, popularly known in the 1880s and 1890s as Sycamore Flat, was part of the Cowell home ranch.[2] Today it is the only part of Pogonip that borders on the San Lorenzo River.

The auto camp and resort at Sycamore Grove was built and managed by Philip Fridley and his wife, Ethel. They leased the approximately ten acres of land from S. H. "Harry" Cowell and later, after his death, from the S. H. Cowell Foundation. Family lore says that Harry Cowell did not want to take money from Philip, but when pressed said he would take no more than one dollar ($1) a month. He also promised that Philip could rent the grove "in perpetuity" as long as a Fridley family member was the lessee. The agreement was confirmed by a handshake between Cowell and Philip Fridley around 1908.[3]

Postcard showing the sign that was suspended from one of a pair of sycamore trees that still mark the entrance to Sycamore Grove. Text on the back: "Camp store at this resort camp in beautiful San Lorenzo Valley, two miles from Santa Cruz beach." (Ronnie Trubek collection)

The Fridley Family

Philip Fridley's father Alonzo Fridley moved to Santa Cruz from Seneca County, New York in 1874 when he was 21 years old. He started out as a tanner for Kirby's Tannery. Later he acquired almost 15 acres of land at the top of Bay Street and started a poultry ranch. He was industrious in this business and was called the "founder of Santa Cruz's commercial poultry industry."[4]

Alonzo Fridley was related to some of the better-known Santa Cruz families through his wife, Salome. Salome's mother, Mary Ann Morgan, was the sister of Judge William Blackburn, an early pioneer who arrived in California in 1845, settling in Santa Cruz soon thereafter, and becoming an Alcalde in 1847. Mary Ann, with her husband James Morgan, their three daughters, and two sons, came later to Santa Cruz, arriving in October 1852. Salome's sister Margaret married Thomas J. Weeks, another Santa Cruz pioneer; and her sister Mary Jane married William H. Rulofson, an early and important photographer of Santa Cruz and San Francisco.[5]

Before marrying Alonzo Fridley in 1877, Salome had married Charles N. Lincoln in May of 1866. Lincoln was a livery-stable owner, known as the "Boy Sheriff" because he had been the youngest sheriff in California, elected to office at the age of 26. Salome's marriage to Lincoln was not a happy one. In an unusual move for that time, she divorced him even though they had two daughters.[6]

Alonzo Fridley married Mrs. Salome Lincoln in December of 1877. Theirs was a happy marriage. Salome who "had long been noted as a horsewoman and lover of animals," thrived on the Fridley ranch with its horses and cows and other pets, as well as the chickens they raised commercially. Salome and Alonzo Fridley had three sons, Philip, Elmer, and Herbert. They all grew up in the rural atmosphere of the time along with Salome's two daughters from her first marriage: Gertrude and Marie Lincoln. Their granddaughter Phyllis later spoke of idyllic visits to the family ranch, the wonderful food

Detail from a 1923 map showing the relation of Alonzo Fridley's chicken ranch at 240 Bay Street to the Cowell ranch house on High Street. Dotted lines added to show present route of Bay Drive. What was Bay St. is now Cardiff Place. Today Fridley Drive passes through what was the Fridley ranch. (Adapted from map published by Arthur M. Baldwin, Map Room, University Library, UC Santa Cruz)

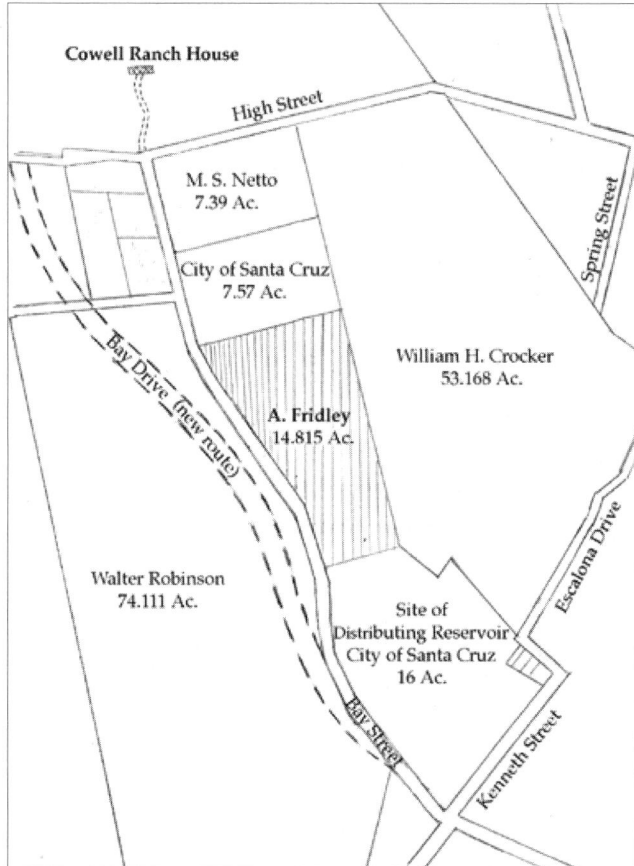

Cowell Ranch House

High Street

M. S. Netto
7.39 Ac.

City of Santa Cruz
7.57 Ac.

Spring Street

William H. Crocker
53.168 Ac.

Bay Drive (new route)

A. Fridley
14.815 Ac.

Walter Robinson
74.111 Ac.

Escalona Drive

Site of
Distributing Reservoir
City of Santa Cruz
16 Ac.

Bay Street

Kenneth Street

The Fridley family marching in the Santa Cruz hills with an American flag, probably July 4, 1918. Ethel carrying the flag; Philip holding baby Robert; Phyllis facing camera with Ernest talking to her; grandmother Roselle Redding and Vernon on the right. (Sharon Christensen collection)

and the kindness of Alonzo and Salome.[7]

Philip Fridley was born July 22, 1882. As a boy he would ride his horse out to Sycamore Flat. The flat ran along the San Lorenzo River where there were many beautiful swimming holes and where the fishing was good. He fell in love with this spot and dreamed of living there some day.[8] Philip Fridley and Harry Cowell, whose family owned Sycamore Flat, were reported to be good friends. Certainly the two families knew each other. The Fridley chicken ranch was very close to the Cowell family home off High Street.

Philip Fridley married Ethel Redding in 1906. She had recently arrived in Santa Cruz with her father, Ernest Edwin Redding, and her mother, Rosella Tupper. They came to Santa Cruz from Minnesota where Ethel was born. Ernest Redding was a cooper who owned a barrel factory in Minnesota; he was reputed to be "well-to-do."[9] Philip and Ethel had a quiet and private wedding on the morning of April 24, 1906 at her parents' house on Bay Street, followed by an elaborate wedding breakfast. They had originally planned to go to San Francisco for their wedding trip but the earthquake interfered and instead they "spent their honeymoon at Del Monte…They were driven to the train depot in an automobile!"[10]

Philip and his bride settled down in Santa Cruz, building a house at 156 King Street, on the corner of Walnut Street. Although Philip put on a suit and went to work as a salesman for Leask's, Morris Abrams', and Eberts' department stores, he had not forgotten his dream of living at Sycamore Flat. The automobile had changed the type of vacation travelers wanted. "Variations of the tent camp…and cabins with room to park the family automobile became increasingly sought after."[11] With this in mind, Fridley made plans for an auto camp and resort where visitors could drive in, live in tents or cabins, and enjoy the peace of the river and the cool shade of the sycamore trees.

Sycamore Grove Camp, The Beginning

Philip did not open the camp for business until the summer of 1921. In the intervening years, he cleared brush, built roads, and laid down the plumbing and electricity for the campsites. During that time Ethel and Philip Fridley had five children: four sons and

Postcard (postmarked July 15, 1924) showing the dance platform under the sycamore trees. Tents can be seen in the background. (Rick Hyman collection)

Dancers of the late '40s or early '50s on the dance platform. (Dennis Redmond collection)

one daughter. Vernon and Ernest, the eldest sons, were born in 1907 and 1908 respectively. Phyllis was born in 1913. Shortly after Phyllis was born, the family moved from King Street out to Sycamore Grove, but not to a house. For ten years they lived in a big army tent, with several rooms and wooden floors. The two younger boys Robert and Daniel were born during this time, probably in 1917 and 1918, respectively.[12]

The campsites where guests pitched tents were located along the roads Philip had built. In the early days, guests camped in their own tents or in tents supplied by the Fridleys. Each campsite had a hose bib to supply water, a picnic table, and a fire pit for bonfires. Soon Philip began building cabins. Eventually, nineteen cabins provided additional and more permanent vacation homes.

From the beginning, entertainment at the camp consisted of swimming and fishing and shuffleboard in the daytime, and dances and bonfires at night. The shuffleboard court was so popular guests often reserved the poles up to a week ahead of time. One of the first structures Philip Fridley built was a dance platform with railings. The platform was lighted from above with Japanese lanterns. Its surface was made of green-painted asphalt over wooden flooring, which softened the thud of dancing feet. He installed hidden floodlights that lit the crowns of the sycamore trees above the dance floor. The music came from a jukebox that played five songs for a nickel. Surely many a summer romance began around this dance platform.[13]

A large communal fire pitt was at the far end of the platform. Here Philip would build huge bonfires using five-foot logs of sycamore and tanoak. As described by Vernon Fridley, Jr., one of Philip's grandsons, "The sparks disappeared in the tree crowns far above. Adults in family clans talked and laughed and occasionally a song was started and picked up by all. If singing continued Grandpa turned the jukebox to 'low'." The Fridleys were teetotalers, so drinking was discouraged at the Grove. Late nights were also discouraged. By eleven, all the fires were doused and the campers were expected to be safely in their tents or cabins.[14]

The River

Dancing, bonfires and shuffleboard added to the joy of the camp, but it was the river that drew the thousands of guests to Sycamore Grove. Campers spent their days swimming in the river, having

Postcard of a swimming hole at the south end of Sycamore Grove Camp.
(Sharon Christensen collection)

water fights, making sand castles on the sandy beaches, and catching crawdads in nets. In season, the river provided runs of steelhead, silver salmon, and trout.

The San Lorenzo enters Sycamore Grove at its northeast corner where it runs headlong into a solid rock outcrop. The river then turns south, falling into a deep pool. Philip Fridley hung a rope and tire swing high on a redwood tree overlooking the pool for the more adventurous kids to swing on and then drop into the river. The very young children would swim from beaches at shallower stretches further south along the river. Rafters could go down the river, entering at the deep pool.

In the winter when the water was high and ran brown from the rains, the steelhead returned from the ocean, resting on their journey in the big pools of the river. At that time, the hole at the north end of Sycamore Grove became a popular place not only for the camp residents but also for the local fishermen. The opening of fishing season would find six or eight fishermen there at daylight and up to a dozen more by ten in the morning.[15]

Building Continued

Sometime after they moved to their tent in the grove, Philip Fridley built a sprawling board and batten one-story house where the family could live comfortably year round. This house would be the center of family activity for years to come. It was located at the

97

Ethel Fridley, on the left, and her friend Minnie Silva holding a steelhead caught in the San Lorenzo River at Sycamore Grove. (Sharon Christensen collection)

left of the camp entrance across from the camp store and office—in the early days, the house also served as the camp office.

A second building, separated from the main house by a covered driveway, was used for storage. This is where the Fridleys kept canvas for the tents, lumber, kegs of tar and nails, extra mattresses, sheets, blankets and pillows, an old white dump truck, and the bicycle Philip used to patrol the campground[16]

Philip Fridley later built a small two-room building to the right of the camp entrance. This building held the store in front and the camp office in the back. The store had a cooler for drinks and milk, a display of postcards, and other sundries campers might want. A pair of gas pumps provided gas for the family and for guests. When the store was open in the summer, residents of Paradise Park were known to walk down for milk and popsicles. The keys to the cabins were kept on a board in the back room, which served as the office. The office bathroom key also hung on this board below a sign that said "Three At A Time Only."[17]

As soon as the family house and the store were built, Philip began building cabins. Each cabin had its own small fire pit. Many of the cabins were near the store, main house and dance floor. Three cabins were built on the hillside behind the house; and three more were built at the end of the northern road near the deep swimming hole. The southernmost area of the campground was primarily devoted to camping sites. Some sites had tent cabins; others had only a picnic table, a water pipe and a fire pit.

A cluster of three large cabins, each with three rooms, heat, and plumbing were built into the hillside on an upper road behind the Fridley's house. These cabins were available for the occasional winter visitor or for members of the Fridley family who sometimes stayed

Postcard showing the house the Fridley's built for themselves. In the early years, the office was in the back of the smaller section on the right. The kitchen ran across the front of the back section and the bedrooms were behind the kitchen. Notice the stone walls ending in parapets.
(Ronnie Trubek collection)

Postcard (postmarked July 25, 1937) shows two children walking on "North Drive" leading from the swimming hole. A typical cabin on the right; notice the garage doors next to front door. (Photo by Harry A. Kay; Rick Hyman collection)

Sycamore Grove Camp sketched from memory by Philip Tuma and Sharon Christensen, grandchildren of Philip and Ethel Fridley, with help from an aerial photograph..

The large hillside cabins, each with three rooms, heat and plumbing, and parking underneath, stood on the road above the Fridley's house. (Photo by Robert Laws; Ronnie Trubek collection)

at the camp after they were grown. Other cabins were built along the north road and between the highway and the south road. Additional campsites were available along the north road.

A concrete building near the river housed the laundry and showers. Guests would sign up for the showers. A large burner near the highway provided a place to burn leaves. Raking and burning the large sycamore leaves was an ongoing task at the camp. "The blacktopped parts and graveled roads needed to be raked and cleared daily. What a job!" recalls Sharon Christensen.[18]

The War Years

Sycamore Grove Camp had done well during the depression because it provided an inexpensive vacation. Campers brought their own food and activities cost very little extra. But when the United States entered World War II, fewer campers came. Gas was rationed and vacations were curtailed for those with essential jobs. Those campers who did come reported that they just wanted to get away from the war. They danced and told tales around the fire pit. Floodlights lit the crowns of the massive sycamores "making a golden-green heaven above and a feeling of being in a safe place."[19]

101

During the 1930s, the Fridley children were still living at the grove. But by 1939, most were grown and had moved out. Vernon attended forestry school in Oregon until he returned to Santa Cruz to work as a PG&E lineman; Ernest married and stayed in Santa Cruz, working as a telephone lineman; Phyllis married and moved to Sacramento, though she soon returned to Santa Cruz; Robert was attending Salinas Junior College (now Hartnell); and Daniel enlisted in the navy in 1939. During the depression, when times grew hard, Vernon and Phyllis brought their families home to Sycamore Grove for brief stays. It was good that the family home was large and the hillside cabins available.[20]

When the United States entered World War II, Robert enlisted in the U. S. Air Force. After his training, Robert was sent to Fogge in the south of Italy where he piloted a B-17 bomber, a "Flying Fortress." Daniel was an aviation machinist's mate stationed in Hawaii when the Japanese attacked Pearl Harbor. Later, he was assigned to a "Black Cat" PBY-Catalina Patrol Squadron. Vernon and Ernest had war-essential jobs and were frozen in them for the duration.[21]

In June of 1944, Philip and Ethel received word that Robert was missing in action. Lieutenant Robert Fridley was bringing his badly damaged plane back to Italy from his 23rd mission when he fatally crashed off the coast of Yugoslavia. The following year his parents were presented posthumously with the Air Medal and two Oak Leaf clusters "For meritorious achievement in aerial flight while participating in sustained operational activities against the enemy."[22]

Daniel, in the south Pacific, fared better. Although his Black Cat squadron fought at Guadalcanal, he survived the war. Back in 1942,

Campers gather at the fire pit; the dance platform to their right.
(Dennis Redmond collection)

when he was 22 years old, he wrote home, "I sure would like to be at [Sycamore Grove] and have a big fire in the pit with about three dozen flank steaks sizzling on the grate, hot French bread, big salad, beer, strawberry shortcake – whipped cream and everything like we used to years ago. Well, I can think about it anyway, can't I?"[23]

above: The car dates this postcard as post World War II. The camp store is on the right, the picnic area on the left. (Sharon Christensen collection)
below: Brisk business in inner tubes for rafting at the store. (Dennis Redmond collection)

A Devastating Flood

After the war, Philip and Ethel Fridley continued to manage Sycamore Grove. They no longer lived full-time at the grove, but had bought a duplex in Santa Cruz at 115 Grover Lane. They made a winter home in one half and rented out the other half.

Then disaster struck. On December 22, 1955, an unusually heavy rainfall caused the San Lorenzo River to rise rapidly. The river, which normally ran with four feet of water in a 100-foot wide channel, was up to 22 feet in a channel double its normal width. By the early hours of December 23, the river was eleven feet deep in downtown Santa Cruz; by daylight it was up to fourteen feet. A third of Santa Cruz was completely inundated.[24]

The night of December 22, Philip Fridley was at his home on Grover Lane. Hearing of the rising river, he rushed over to Sycamore Grove to see what he could do. Unfortunately, the strain was too much

Photo in the *Santa Cruz Sentinel*, December 27, 1955, with the caption: "Sycamore Grove, one of the more popular summer resorts along the usually placid San Lorenzo river resembles a log jam following the flood." Notice the summer cabin torn from its foundation among the topsy-turvy wreckage.

for his 73-year-old heart. In an attempt to save his camp, he suffered a heart attack and died in a local hospital the following morning.[25]

The whole San Lorenzo Valley suffered heavily in the flood. Among the many casualties was Sycamore Grove, which was devastated. Wally Trabing went up to see the damage and, in an article published December 25, reported that Sycamore Grove was "a sea of oozing mud and scrambled cabins. The small units were scattered like building blocks."[26]

After the flood, Ethel Fridley carried on. With help from her family, she had the debris cleared away and cleaned up the cabins that were still standing. Somehow, she managed to keep Sycamore Grove Camp going for almost ten years. Like her husband before her, she paid the Cowell Foundation the rent every month a few days before it was due. But, in 1964 when she was 76 years old, she wanted to quit. The rent was no longer the $1 a month agreed to in 1908. Between 1950 and 1955, the rent was $50 a month; in 1956 the Cowell Foundation raised it to $75 a month. By 1964 it had probably risen again.[27] In 1961 the Cowell Foundation had received an outside offer to buy the grove and continue operating the resort.[28] The foundation was apparently not interested in selling and continued loyal to Harry Cowell's commitment to the Fridley family.

Ethel looked for a family member who could take over. Her granddaughter, Sharon, with her new husband, Larry Christensen, came to the rescue. They agreed to help her run the grove and kept it open the summer of 1964. That year only a few paying campers stayed at Sycamore Grove; most summer tourists to Santa Cruz now stayed at chain motels near the beach.[29] When Ethel Fridley died April 15, 1968 at her home on Grover Lane, aged 80, the camp at the grove was no longer in operation.[30]

The cabins and other infrastructure were removed by the mid 1970s. In 1989 when the City of Santa Cruz took over the property from the Cowell Foundation, it was once again a jungle of poison oak, blackberries, and fallen trees. Only a few stone walls and the cement shuffleboard platform remain today as reminders of the once thriving resort.

Poster designed by Mark Primack in 1977 calling on Santa Cruz citizens to join the Greenbelt Committee to Preserve Pogonip. (Paul Lee collection)

Chapter Eleven

Pogonip And The City

Annexation of Pogonip

In 1977, a proposal was in the air to have the City of Santa Cruz purchase the Pogonip land and annex it to the city. Pogonip was the largest area of open space near the city, which had an urgent need for housing. The Cowell Foundation, for its part, was anxious to make some money from Pogonip and wanted to sell.

City Planning Commission chairman, Gerald Bowden proposed that the 614 Pogonip acres be acquired from the Cowell Foundation as part of the city's general plan. He further proposed that the city inaugurate a resale program while keeping some control over the choice of occupancy. This proposal would mean lots of houses on the Pogonip land and roads running through it. Only one of the seven commissioners, Betsy Darrow, objected to the proposal. She preferred that Live Oak be annexed.[1]

This was not the first time that annexation of land to the City of Santa Cruz had been proposed, nor was it the boldest. Back in 1960, the city proposed increasing its size by four to five times. An Annexation subcommittee of the City Planning Commission and City Council projected a city that included almost the entire county:

> North from Wilder Ranch at the Coast Road to Empire Grade – northeast to Felton – east to Skypark Airport (north end of) – northeast to Bethany Park – north then east to top of Vine Hill on Hwy #17 – south down Blackburn Gulch Road to Mountain View Road and Laurel Glen Road to St. Clare's Retreat – east to the top of Hinckley Ridge (township boundary) – thence down Aptos Creek to Monterey Bay.[2]

But times had changed since 1960 and in the late 1970s the much smaller Pogonip annexation proposal had many vocal opponents. By March of 1978, foes of the annexation plan organized and prepared to fight. Environmentalists by the hundreds attended the first public hearing on the new general plan in order to protest the Pogonip annexation. They formed a Greenbelt Committee to Preserve Pogonip and presented petitions with, they claimed, 1,700 signatures. Gary Patton, county supervisor representing the city and fresh from his triumph against development of Lighthouse Field, drew the biggest applause. To a standing ovation, he concluded, "If we believe that by manifest destiny we must destroy Pogonip in the name of planning then we will be victimized by the future rather than be its creator." The Commission pledged to consider all the comments at a study session on April 6.[3]

At that Commission study session, the Greenbelt Committee sat silently as the Planning Department presented the city's general plan, which still included annexation of Pogonip's 614 acres for development. Soon the plan would be presented to the City Council.[4] Then in May, *Sentinel* writer Wally Trabing stepped in, devoting a column to this issue. To quote from that column:

> Now, there is a move afoot to eventually smear the Pogonip greenbelt with houses and streets and a shopping center. It is owned by the Cowell Foundation, which wants to sell it. Those who forget past mistakes suffer by the repetition of them. The mistake in this case would be to remove this jewel from our sylvan crown. It is also human nature to forget that all these areas of beauty so coveted today, from Yosemite to our own beaches and parks, are the result of long public struggles. The seed of such a struggle already has been planted to save Pogonip.[5]

At a study session held by the City Council in early June, the annexation was discussed for well over an hour. No one denied that the city faced a housing crisis. But a member of a UC Santa Cruz student group, who had studied the issue, remarked that developing the city's last nearby environmental resource would be "like throwing your last log onto the fire in the face of a blizzard." Councilman Joe Ghio asked, "Why should we give up the treasure to provide recreation to Santa Clara Valley."[6] Celia Scott (then, Celia Von der Muhll), urged preservation of the land. Like Wally Trabing, she referred to Pogonip as "the jewel" of the city.[7]

Measures J and O To The Rescue

This was the background when, in June 1978, county voters overwhelmingly passed Measure J, a strict countywide growth control ordinance authored by County supervisor Gary Patton. Patton had been elected overwhelmingly in 1974 by a group of environmentally concerned voters, many of them students or former students at UC Santa Cruz. (Ballots cast for him on campus were an overwhelming 1,832 to 17!) Measure J required supervisors to establish a measure that restricted the number of available building permits, to develop an annual growth rate, to ensure that 15 percent of all housing was affordable, to protect agricultural lands, and to concentrate development in urban areas. This last restriction was the one that affected Pogonip.[8]

The next step was an even more restrictive ordinance. Santa Cruz city initiative, Measure O the so-called "greenbelt initiative," was passed in the 1979 city election. Measure O added a provision to establish a greenbelt around the city that would remain in effect until 1990. The greenbelt would consist of about 3,000 acres both inside and outside the city limits. It would restrict expansion of city services into these greenbelt zones. The greenbelt would include all of Pogonip.

This greenbelt initiative was very controversial. Attorneys for the city foresaw problems defending the measure in court and the City Council opposed it.[9] The group promoting Measure O, whose slogan was "Save Pogonip," had to appeal to the State Court of

Gerald Bowden was Planning Commission chairman during the uproar over the plans to annex Pogonip to the city. Later, as Assistant City Attorney, Bowden was responsible for defending Measure O in the numerous lawsuits against the city. (Dan Coyro)

Appeals to put the measure on the ballot. But when it was presented to city voters in 1980, the measure passed overwhelmingly with 82 percent voting yes.[10] It was clear that this measure would effectively stop development of Pogonip—that is if it survived the legal challenges of its opponents.

In early 1980, lawsuits against the city proliferated. The main suit was by the S. H. Cowell Foundation. It pressed a claim for ten million dollars unless the city overturned Measure O to allow "reasonable development of Pogonip along multipurpose lines." This was a blow to the city. As the Cowell lawyer pointed out, the Cowells had a history of generosity to Santa Cruz County and the Cowell Foundation still owned the entire Pogonip area outside the city and some 60 acres within the city.[11] Two years later in April of 1982, the Cowell Foundation dropped its lawsuit, but left a legal door open to pursue it in the future. They preferred conciliation to litigation.

The Pogonip Citizen's Advisory Committee

In 1984, Max Thelen Jr., the president of the Cowell Foundation, formed a fifteen-member committee: The Pogonip Citizen's Advisory Committee. The Cowell Foundation was represented on the committee by William Plageman, Jr., an attorney for the foundation and by Stephanie Hauk, who was hired to help coordinate the committee meetings. Stephanie Hauk was experienced in county politics, having been an aide to state senator Henry Mello and to county Supervisors Dale Dawson and Robley Levy.

The committee members were purposely chosen to represent a wide range of interests. They included environmentalists (David Bockman of the Sierra Club and Celia Scott-Von der Muhll); developers (Don Fultz, who once wanted to put thousands of homes on the Wilder Ranch); local businessmen (Gary Reese and Charlene Shaffer of the Chamber of Commerce, and Norman Lezin, former mayor and owner of Salz Tannery); representatives from UC Santa Cruz (Julia Armstrong and Paul Niebanck); representatives of local government (Andrew Schiffrin, aide to Supervisor Patton, Linda Wilshusen, executive director of the Regional Transportation Commission, and former mayor Lorette Wood); and Lloyd Williams, a trustee of the Santa Cruz County Land Trust. As liaisons to the local Planning Departments, City Planning Director, Peter Katzlberger, and County Planning Director, Kris Schenk, were non-voting members.

The committee hoped these representatives of various special-interest groups could arrive at a consensus about the future of Pogonip. Stephanie Hauk hoped to keep politics to a minimum and to develop "trust and understanding." The Cowell Foundation, she said, would abide by the wishes of the community, but only if they could realize a fair return on their property. Cowell was "not interested in handing it over to the city." The foundation needed to generate some income from the property for their many charitable activities. Hauk reiterated that Cowell was asking the community "to work with them in deciding what is in the future for the property."[12]

Plans For Pogonip

In May of 1986, after two years of brainstorming, the committee announced it was ready to present its findings at public hearings. At this time, development was still an option—though on only 50 to 70 acres. Ideas for possible development included housing or a conference center of some kind; a campsite for the homeless proposed by Peter Carota, operator of the St. Francis Soup Kitchen; a performing arts center suggested by the Cultural Council; a botanical garden suggested by Paul Lee, former UC Santa Cruz professor and horticulturalist. Other possibilities included a golf course or a park with a network of trails.[13]

In discussing their progress so far, Stephanie Hauk, ever the optimist, reported that committee members had not yet reached a consensus but were closing in on it, hoping to reach a decision by the beginning of 1987. Stephanie Hauk remained proud of the committee. She said they had "stuck this out on a volunteer basis for over two years" and only one person, the developer Don Fultz, had dropped out.[14]

In February of 1987, the committee was still undecided. They considered a ballot measure asking the city to buy the property for an open space or parks district. The Cowell Foundation "hasn't grown impatient yet," but if voters decided neither to buy nor develop the property, Cowell might be forced to "consider other options" such as selling to a private party, "waiting for the political winds to change," or entering into a joint venture with the university. The university needed more room for student and faculty housing and was interested in a new eastern access to the campus.[15]

Eastern Access

The elephant in the room throughout these discussions was the question of an eastern access road to UC Santa Cruz. In 1961 when the university was in the early planning stages, the county entered into a contract with the University of California regents. In that contract they agreed to build a six-lane highway to provide eastern access to the University. The agreement stated, in part:

> County shall, at its expense, provide right of way and engineering and construct and maintain a connecting highway in the vicinity of the junction of State Highway 9, 17, and 1, and a point on the eastern perimeter of the campus area, which point shall be approved by the University. County further agrees that the right of way acquired will be of sufficient width ultimately to accommodate a six traveled lane roadway with a divided center strip.[16]

Since that original contract was signed, the proposed road size was reduced to two lanes, no date for construction was set, and the ultimate student population size was reduced. Rather than setting a date for construction, the contract called for it to be built "when the necessity arises."[17] Still, the question kept coming up . Several routes were suggested but, whatever the route, it would have to go through some part of Pogonip. And, because any road would open Pogonip up to development, the question of eastern access was a red flag to local environmentalists.

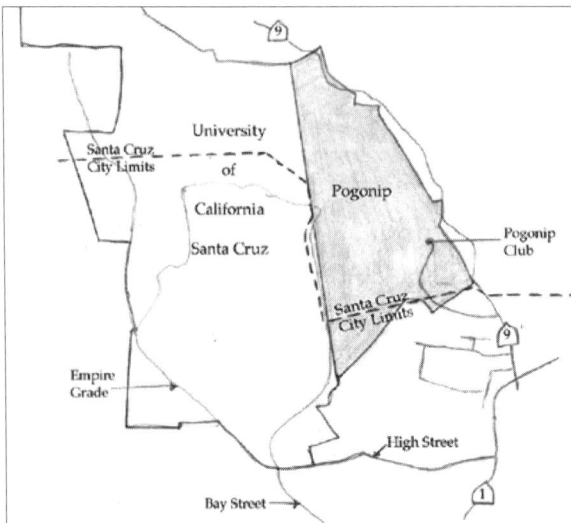

Relation of Pogonip to UC Santa Cruz, the city of Santa Cruz, and highways 1 and 9. An eastern access road would need to cross through Pogonip, probably through the lower or central portion, as the upper portion is steep and heavily wooded. At this time, before the city's acquisition, most of Pogonip was outside the city limits.

The Cowell Foundation, when asked if they were interested in a deal with UC Santa Cruz to use Pogonip for an eastern access, replied with a decisive "no." Nevertheless, at least one committee member wanted the question of eastern access to come up. "If someone doesn't bring it up, I will," said Linda Wilshusen of the Regional Transportation Commission. Stephanie Hauk assured everyone that such a road is only one of many ideas being investigated.[18]

State Bond Provides a Solution

In March of 1987, the Cowell Foundation, having grown weary of waiting for a solution, presented the people of Santa Cruz with a figure for which they would sell the Pogonip land. They asked $15 million, which Cowell representative William Plageman, Jr. said was a "major concession to the real value of Pogonip."[19] Would the city be able to come up with this money? Due to lucky timing, the answer lay in a statewide "parks and wildlife" bond to be placed on the ballot in June of 1988.

Andrew Schiffrin who had been a member of the Pogonip Advisory Committee for its two-year tenure, commented that the two main accomplishments of the committee were: 1) getting Cowell to set a price on the land and 2) setting in motion the process of putting the state park bond measure on the ballot.[20]

The state park bond measure was put on the ballot by an initiative drafted by the Planning and Conservation League. This was unusual; in most cases bonds are presented by the legislature. A wide variety of other groups joined the PCL in supporting the initiative. In April the members of the Pogonip Citizen's Advisory Committee unanimously endorsed the inclusion of Pogonip in the proposed initiative. In May, members of the Santa Cruz Chamber of Commerce spoke up in favor of the initiative. There seemed to be no organized opposition.[21]

Three hundred seventy five thousand signatures were needed to place the initiative on the ballot. By November of 1987, local organizers of the Californians for Parks and Wildlife Initiative turned in box loads of petitions collected within the county that contained more than 21,000 signatures. Statewide, over 725,000 signatures were collected. The initiative was placed on the ballot in June of 1988.[22]

The stated purpose of the initiative, Proposition 70, was to authorize a general obligation bond of $776,000,000 to acquire, develop, rehabilitate, protect or restore California park, wildlife, coastal, and natural lands. Of particular interest to Santa Cruz was the inclusion in the initiative of the following text:

> Fifteen million dollars ($15,000,000) for acquisition of those greenbelt lands known as the Pogonip property located in the City of Santa Cruz and the County of Santa Cruz, as defined in the 1979 City of Santa Cruz Greenbelt Ordinance. This acquisition shall be accomplished through grants to the following entities listed in order of priority: (1) the City of Santa Cruz and (2) a park and open-space district or a park and recreation district formed by the local electorate.

If passed, the bond would provide the fifteen million dollars needed to purchase Pogonip.[23] Proposition 70, the Wildlife, Coastal, and Park Land Conservation Bond Act Initiative Statute was passed by 68 percent of the electorate. Now the question was: who would use the bond money to buy Pogonip—the city or a recreation district? The decision was easy; the city was already in a position to buy the land, whereas a park and recreation district had not been established.

The City Buys Pogonip

On April 4, 1989, escrow closed on the property. Pogonip's 614 acres were now officially the property of the City of Santa Cruz. The Cowell Foundation received $14.9 million and the state kept $100,000 for administering the sale. Fortunately, there was money in the city budget to pay for maintenance, primarily for private security guards to patrol the land where illegal camping had been a problem.[24]

The next big issue was what would the city do with this acquisition. The very diversity of the land, with open meadows and hidden pockets of forest presented both opportunities and problems for future use. The property could lend itself both to wilderness use and community activities. Santa Cruz Parks and Recreation Department director, Jim Lang, was the man in charge of planning for the future of Pogonip. He pointed out the bond issue said only that the land was to be used for public open space, leaving a lot of latitude and that "Just about any outdoor recreational use could be considered appropriate." He went on to mention parks, a swimming pool, polo grounds, a golf course, and a conference center as possibilities.[25]

The question of what to do with this beautiful and diverse property would occupy the people of Santa Cruz for years to come.

Panoramic view of the Pogonip lands now the property of the City of Santa Cruz.
(Don Fukuda)

Chapter Twelve

The Clubhouse Controversy

Problems With the Clubhouse

Two years before the city took over ownership of the Pogonip land, the Pogonip Club had suffered a serious setback when the county condemned their clubhouse. At that time, the clubhouse still belonged to the Cowell Foundation. William Plageman, Jr., of the law firm of Thelen, Marrin, Johnson, & Bridges, who was the Cowell spokesman, said they were working with engineers and Pogonip Club leaders to determine the full extent of the damage. Cowell was the owner, but the Pogonip Club had just negotiated a 28-year lease on the clubhouse and its surrounding two and one half acres. One of the stipulations of the lease was that the club renovate the clubhouse. Together Pogonip and Cowell had to decide how to do this.

In May of 1987, an engineering firm submitted a report to William Plageman, Jr. The report was signed by Robert L. Schwein, Civil Engineer of Schwein/Christensen Engineering, Ltd. It was also signed by Larry Pearson, City Planner, and Jim Foster, Board Chair of the club.[1] The report suggested various schemes for restoring the clubhouse and included estimated costs. Part of the report was the engineer's assessment of the damage:

#1   [text missing – probably referred to Fireplace]   Long-Term, High Pressure on soil under fireplace has compressed that soil more than other areas. Water and space has been squeezed out from between soil grains over a long period of time. Fireplace & its foundation have subsided. Check plumbness of chimney. Enlarge & Deepen Foundation – more centered under chimney (crack near firebox doesn't appear "structural")

#2   Exterior Wall Foundations NOT Wide or Deep Enough AND Exterior Studwalls below main floor damaged by decay and insects.

Temporarily support floor joists near exterior walls and first row of interior footings. Remove Exterior studwalls and existing concrete – REPLACE, REFRAME INTERIOR – Girders do not appear to comply with 85 code.
<u>Work to Floor Level at Fireplace</u>

#3 Vaulted (Cathedral) Ceiling in Great Room Sagging and pushing front wall outward at top.
JACK UP RIDGE OF CATHEDRAL CEILING AND PLUMB WALLS (Probably remove Porch Roof first)
Add to Existing rafters to meet 85 code.

#4 [text missing here - probably refers to code failures]
Fire-resistive construction, and low-flame-spread-rated interior floor, wall & ceiling finishes. (Also Fire-retardant roof covering) Energy requirements and handicapped provisions will also apply, electrical, plumbing & mechanical codes will incur upgrade, "Historical" listing may soften requirements, but only slightly, A Fire sprinkler system will also be required.

#5 Planning Department will probably have objection to "Residential" use of the upper story. Almost any other use allowable within Planning Regulations would incur heavier floor loading, one-hour construction, a second exit, upgrade Electrical, Plumbing & Mechanical.
Suggest only a small mezzanine be retained – if any of the second story must be retained. If unusable space, one-hour not needed, and rear roof could be reshaped to match front.
Since not on the Historical List this modification should be most readily acceptable to Planning Department, and should also save much processing time as well as construction time and cost.

#6 Present-day Kitchen Equipment could be installed during "down-time" and reallocation of all "accessory space" could easily be incorporated in the work, without significant increase – if any of down time.

This assessment was accompanied by four "schemes" with their estimated costs:

<u>SCHEME #1</u> – MINIMUM STRUCTURAL UPGRADE
This plan would provide structural upgrading by converting the open framed stub walls between the foundation and the shear walls by adding plywood sheathing. At the first floor, walls and roof loads of the first floor level. Tie downs would also be incorporated. Six roof trusses would be added to the distressed ceiling in the main room to tie the front wall to the

rear portion of the frame and to re-support the roof.
Estimated Cost: $200,000

SCHEME #2 – MINIMUM STRUCTURAL UPGRADE INCLUDING UTILIZING SECOND FLOOR

This plan would involve all of Scheme #1 plus structural work on the second floor so that it can be utilized. Additionally, the exterior building surfaces would be reworked to be watertight. Ten new shear walls would be added to the second floor.
Estimated Cost: $350,000

SCHEME #3 – COMPLETE UPGRADE

This plan would include all of Scheme #2 plus fire protection, mechanical, electrical, and kitchen upgrading.
Estimated Cost: 8,500 sq.ft. x $100/sq.ft. = $850,000

SCHEME #4 – ALL NEW STRUCTURE

It may be possible to salvage some or all of the foundation and fireplace; however, it would probably make demolition much more costly.
Estimated Cost: 8,500 sq.ft. x $75-100/sq.ft. = $640,000 - $850,000

So there it was. Costs to restore the clubhouse ranged from $200,000 to $850,000 and costs to rebuild it from scratch ranged from $640,000 to $850,000. It was now up to Cowell and the board of the Pogonip Club to decide what to do. There must have been many heated discussions, none of which have been recorded. One thing is clear; by the time the City of Santa Cruz took over ownership of Pogonip, the issue of the clubhouse was still very much up in the air.

The Pogonip Club, which had the greatest interest in fixing up the clubhouse, put Board Chairman Jim Foster in charge of repackaging the former showplace. Foster and the long-suffering club members would have their work cut out for them. At that time, according to Foster, their mandate was "to restore the building and grounds so that it would look exactly the way it did in the beginning." In 1989 he estimated the renovation could cost upwards of $1 million. To help the club finance the reconstruction, he suggested assessing members $5,000 a year over a three-year period; he added, "We're trying to make it as affordable as possible."[2]

Historic Landmark

In July of 1989, Colleen McInerney-Meagher, who was an original member of the Pogonip Polo Club and an honorary member of the current Pogonip Club, wrote to the Santa Cruz City Historic

Preservation Commission requesting Historic Landmark Designation for the clubhouse. She hoped the unique exterior of the building would be preserved through such a designation. One unusual architectural feature of the clubhouse was the use of unstripped redwood poles for the porch. Colleen asked that, "As the last surviving remnant of Pogonip's historic past...this architecturally and historically significant building [should] be accorded all the possible protections and recognition it so rightly deserves."[3]

In October 1989 she wrote again, this time to the Santa Cruz City Council. And, again in November of that year she wrote the Historic Landmark Commission, enclosing a copy of the Historic Resources Inventory. This inventory listed the Pogonip Clubhouse, described it, and summarized its history.[4] She again urged the Historic Preservation Commission to designate the clubhouse a Historic Landmark. The commission apparently delayed their decision at their November 15 meeting, and Colleen wrote once again in January of 1990. This time she enclosed the engineering report submitted to the Cowell Foundation—the report quoted earlier in this chapter.[5] The clubhouse was eventually given a Santa Cruz Historic Landmark Designation, but it was not nominated by the state for the National Register of Historic Places.

A park ranger rides past the Pogonip clubhouse in 1988. (Bill Lovejoy)

In the midst of this controversy, on October 17, 1989, the 6.9 magnitude Loma Prieta earthquake, which demolished large portions of downtown Santa Cruz, caused further damage to the clubhouse.

Club Plans New Clubhouse

In 1990, the Pogonip Club was still without a clubhouse where their members could congregate. It seemed to the club that the best solution was to demolish the existing historic clubhouse and build a new one. In March of 1990, Jeremy Lezin and fellow board member, Jim Foster, both members since childhood, reported to the *Sentinel* that local architects Thatcher and Thompson were working on a design for a new clubhouse. The new clubhouse would include a restaurant and bar open to the public; it would have meeting rooms upstairs; and an outdoor patio that would also be open to the public.[6]

The new building was expected to cost $1 million. To raise the money for this project, the club needed to increase memberships from the current 40 to at least 150. (As recently as 1986, the Pogonip Club had over 180 members). Members, both new and current, would pay a special "secondary" membership fee of $5,000 per family to pay for the new clubhouse. This would be in addition to the current one-time membership fee of $500. Initial monthly dues were raised to $60 per family; membership would be limited to 200 families. The secondary membership fee would be put to good use in a fund earmarked for building a new clubhouse. Members could use the pool and tennis courts until the new clubhouse was built. Thereafter,

James Foster and Jeremy Lezin looking over plans for the new Pogonip clubhouse.
(Dan Coyro)

Architectural rendering of the new clubhouse by Thacher & Thompson; not exactly a replica, but similar in feeling to the original clubhouse. (Brochure issued by the Pogonip Club; undated, but probably 1990)

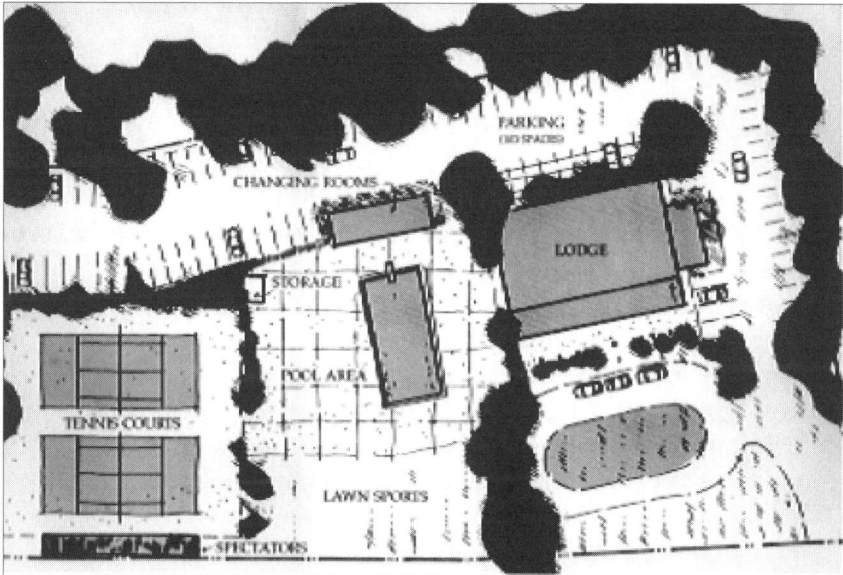

Plan for the revised clubhouse and its environs. (Same brochure and architects as above.)

the members would enjoy all the amenities of the new building.

The club hoped to start construction in the spring of 1991. To entice new members, the club distributed a brochure touting the "new" Pogonip Polo Club as having been in "operation over 80 years."[7] The brochure featured a summary of the clubhouse design proposed by Thacher and Thompson. The design specified:

- A new clubhouse that was "on the outside a replica of the original design" but that inside would have a more open floor plan which would allow members full use of the bar, kitchen, and dining room, even when areas are rented for public functions.
- A new garden with circular driveway allowing "graceful entry to the clubhouse."
- New parking lots behind the clubhouse to keep cars out of view. [Back in the polo days, spectators parked their cars between the clubhouse and the polo field to watch the games from the comfort of their cars.]
- Renovated dressing rooms and bathrooms poolside and a heated pool.
- Improved play area with climbing structures and swings.[8]

Opposition Mounts

These hopeful plans did not go unopposed. No sooner had the Pogonip Club made known its desire to demolish the old clubhouse than Colleen McInerney-Meagher leaped into the fray. A letter published by the *Santa Cruz Sentinel* on April 22, 1990 expressed Colleen's strong opposition to demolishing the historic clubhouse. She noted that the clubhouse had been "placed on the historic survey list and the building also qualifies as a perfect example of a craftsman's bungalow built by a local architect." She claimed it was not the "prerogative of the present Pogonip Club to...destroy an historic landmark."[9]

On September 2, 1990, the *Sentinel* published a Public Notice of "Historic Demolition Permit to demolish the Pogonip Clubhouse. Deletion of the Pogonip clubhouse from the Historic Building Survey. Design Permit and Special Use Permit to construct a new clubhouse structure and site improvements."[10] In response, Douglas Deitch, a local realtor and club member, joined Colleen in the battle to prevent demolition of the clubhouse.

In a long letter to the Santa Cruz City Council, Deitch asked the council to refuse to extend the lease the club held on the Pogonip property, thereby denying them the right to demolish the clubhouse. He pointed out that the club was behind in their rent to the city, that they had not completed their plans to restore the clubhouse within the specified time limit, that these failures were not caused by the recent October 1989 earthquake, and that it would be financially irresponsible of the city to extend the club's lease. Colleen backed Doug up in her own letter to the Santa Cruz County Historical Trust, expressing her fervent desire that they "will not allow this historic and significant building to be destroyed.[11]

To no avail. On January 8, 1991, the City Council extended the lease held by the Pogonip Club despite the club being in arrears on its rent. Several members of the Parks and Recreation Commission urged the council not to extend the deadlines. Vice Mayor Don Lane said the club must meet its new deadlines or "the council would be in a position to re-evaluate use of the land."[12]

Demolition Delayed

The city announced they would hold a meeting on March 20, 1991, at which the Historic Preservation Commission would consider whether the Pogonip clubhouse could be demolished. In October of 1990, the Pogonip Club had commissioned a new engineering report. This report from the firm of Donald C. Urfur & Associates, Inc., concluded that the building was in too poor shape to restore. Specifically, the new report, which was accompanied by a series of 21 photographs, made the following points:

> As the building was built before building codes existed, the strength of the vertical and lateral force resisting system is substantially below the minimum strength required by the current codes. The poorly built structure has resulted in a number of structural failures of the building components. To compound the problem, maintenance of the building has been neglected for some time resulting in serious decay of the primary structural support. The earthquake of October 17, 1989 also, apparently caused some damage to the building and fireplace.

These claims of lack of conformance to building codes, insufficient maintenance, and the effect of the recent earthquake, were serious. The optimism about restoring the building that had prevailed after the previous 1987 report was no longer possible. The

Photo 5 from the engineering report
showing extensive dry rot and
deterioration of joists and beams.
(Donald C. Urfur)

city also hired an engineer who agreed with the club that, "the building had deteriorated to such a state that rehabilitation would be impractical."[13]

In response, Douglas Deitch requested an engineering report from Charles Hall Page, who was notably an expert on historic buildings in Santa Cruz. This report concluded that the clubhouse could be restored. Deitch and Colleen McInerney-Meagher both argued strongly that the city needed to have an Environmental Impact Report (EIR) before it could demolish the building. Deitch claimed the California Environmental Quality Act (CEQA) and the city's own "greenbelt" zoning ordinance (Measure O) both required an EIR.[14]

The city argued they were exempt from an EIR because of a post-earthquake law exempting properties so badly damaged they presented a public safety risk. (This exemption allowed the city to tear down the St. George Hotel.) The Planning Department also concluded an EIR was not needed. As a result, the city planning staff recommended the Historic Preservation Commission approve the demolition.

In a last ditch effort to save the clubhouse, Marti Christoffer, an architect with extensive experience rehabilitating historic houses, wrote to Sara Ray of the Historic Preservation Commission, recommending strongly that the clubhouse be saved. She said, "Too many structures like this have been lost to future generations....

Much of what exists could be restored or renovated for clubhouse use without destroying it."[15] The letter dated March 18, 1991 did not, however, sway the commission.

On March 20, 1991, the Historic Preservation Commission voted 4 to 3 against preserving the "decrepit" Pogonip clubhouse. "You can designate it a landmark all you want, but the building is shot," said commission member Christina Waters. Commission chairwoman, Sara Ray, wanted to preserve the building, "This is the Historic Preservation Commission. We should be acting in favor of preserving a building." Local architectural historian, Sarah Boutelle, was also in favor of preserving the building. But John Lisher, a commission member, pointed out that the club would have to spend an extra $500,000 to $1 million to restore the building. If the club disbanded, the problem would revert to the city, which had no money for the restoration. Lisher concluded, "It's going to end up with a chain-link fence around it and then it's going to disappear.... The community will be better served by having a new structure." At this time, the building was no longer on the city's Historic Building Survey because of its dilapidated condition.[16]

Now that they had permission to demolish the old clubhouse, could they get permission to build a new one? The city Zoning Board had to give its okay. On March 28, the Zoning board denied the proposal for a new clubhouse, saying the city needed more answers about grading, sewer, and parking problems before they would certify that an EIR was not needed. The decision was unanimous even though three members, Brandon Cornell, Cynthia Mathews, and Robert Semas, said they would probably support a new clubhouse in the future.[17]

Then, in May of 1991, a "technical glitch in the public notice process" forced the City Council to reconsider tearing down the clubhouse. The public hearing on March 20, at which the Historic Preservation Commission voted to demolish the clubhouse, had been held only 18 days after public notice of the hearing. The law required 21 days. Only three days, but they were critical. Once again, the fate of the clubhouse was in limbo: it could not be torn down; and it could not be replaced.[18]

Last Days Of The Pogonip Club

In August of 1992, the question of the lease held by the Pogonip Club was again being argued in the city. When Santa Cruz took over ownership of the Pogonip land back in 1989, they inherited a 28-year lease that Jim Foster, Board Chair of the club, had negotiated with the Cowell Foundation. The lease was to continue into 2015. Many groups had plans for the space and objected to the city allowing an "exclusive" private club to hold a lease on land that might serve the city better for other uses, for instance, a new city museum. Michael Di Donato felt so strongly about this issue that he resigned as chairman of the Parks and Recreation Commission. He said, "We want to do everything we can to bring that property back into the public domain."[19]

The city on the other hand recognized that they did not have the money to restore or rebuild the clubhouse. They preferred to leave it in the hands of the Pogonip Club. City Manager Richard Wilson pointed out that the city had more pressing problems on its hands. He said, "It's always a question of priorities. I would hate to suggest what (the city) would stop doing to pay for it.... I don't know where the $1 million for the Pogonip Club building would come from."[20]

The Pogonip Club, for its part, was stepping up its membership drive. They were also trying to live down the label of "exclusive" by posting signs at the bottom of the property on Highway 9 that gave out a phone number for any one interested in joining the club. However, the cost of joining was steep: a $5,000 membership fee in addition to the monthly dues.[21]

At the end of 1992, the city gave its approval to restore the old building. The Pogonip Club accepted that they would not be allowed to build a new clubhouse. Now they were intent on raising money for what they called a "facelift." In the club's agreement with the city, the restored clubhouse restaurant would be open to the public for lunch and would be available for rent to the public. Jeremy Lezin, president of the Pogonip Club, praised the club's emphasis on family activities. He said, "There are clubs that have tennis courts and clubs that have pools, but none have the camaraderie that this one does."[22]

They struggled for a year, but eventually the club realized they could not incur the debt needed to restore the existing historic building. To do that, they needed 200 members. Only one new member had joined and existing membership had now dwindled to

53. At the end of October in 1993, the Pogonip Polo Club, a club that had held a historic presence in Santa Cruz for almost 60 years, was forced to close its doors.[23] The Pogonip Club held a "wake" on a Thursday night in October 1993. The following Sunday they had an afternoon party, a "Final Fling," when past and present members gathered to say goodbye.

In a last unsuccessful, attempt to save the club, Jeremy Lezin wrote to Richard Wilson, the City Manager, asking once again for permission to build the simple one-story structure, that the club could afford. He concluded the letter by saying, "It seems sad to dissolve an historic club because of an old building."[24]

POGONIP CLUB'S FINAL FLING!

Sunday, October 17th = 2:00 p.m.

This is it! Our final party to say good-bye. Come on up with something to barbeque, something to share, and your adult drinks. We'll be emptying the Snack Shack of its goodies, including some burgers and hot dogs for the kiddies.

All past Pogonip members are welcome,so pass the word!

In case of rain, the potluck BBQ will be the following Sunday, October 24th.

ROUND ROBIN TENNIS

still on, but now it won't cost anything to play! Please RSVP to the club ASAP to reserve a space. Maximum 12 players

Flyer announcing the last party at Pogonip
(Museum of Art & History)

127

Chapter Thirteen

The City Makes Plans

Another Task Force

The Santa Cruz greenbelt initiative, Measure O, expired in 1990. This milestone sent a signal that the city needed to plan for the future of Pogonip. Proposition 70, the state initiative, had left loopholes allowing some form of development, as long as the development promoted outdoor recreation.

The planning process began in September of 1991 when the Santa Cruz City Council approved a nine-member task force to consider all the options for Pogonip. The task force members were: Lisa Brewer, Beverly Grova, Woutje Herrick, Victor Kimura, David Le Van, Cathy Puccinelli, William Raffo, Robert Semas, and Peter Scott. On

Museum task force chairman, Robert Stephens, at the far right, leads a tour of the Pogonip property in June 1991.
(Shmuel Thaler)

December 14, they held a meeting at which the public was invited to submit their ideas. The goal of their study would be to "create uses that would provide revenue to the city and recreational opportunities to the public, while not hurting natural habitats."[1]

"Nature enthusiasts, equestrians, hikers, sports league representatives" all came to the first meeting to present their dreams for Pogonip. Sports organizations pushed for soccer and football fields on the old polo field; golfers wanted a golf course; advocates from the Homeless Garden Project wanted a botanical garden that would employ the homeless. A number of local residents asked that the land be untouched—that it be left to the hikers and nature lovers to enjoy as is. Others wanted to allow horses and mountain bikes on Pogonip's trails. The task force promised to respond to these concerns by the fall of 1992.[2]

The Task Force Reports

The task force did its work well. It reported to the public on possible uses of Pogonip at a hearing on October 5, 1992. After the hearing, they would accept written comments until October 16, and following the comment period, would submit their final report to the City Council. The initial report proposed three alternatives:

1) To leave the property as is.
2) To allow multiple uses, including horses and bicycles on trails, a natural history museum, a garden tended by the homeless, the Pogonip Club, and a campground.
3) To add to the second alternative, an 18-hole golf course and playing fields.

Leave Pogonip Alone. This was the cry of those who saw Pogonip as an indispensable refuge from the stress of urban life. Less than a mile from downtown, Pogonip provided a landscape "of lush forest, spring-fed brooks and sun-drenched meadows. Overhead hawks and eagles circle. Below deer graze and bobcats hunt." So Robert Pollie wrote in a *Sentinel* opinion piece. He continued, "We go there to hike, to jog, to picnic, to rest and retreat. In its quiet and seclusion we forget for a while the burdens and vexations of our city lives."[3]

This was also arguably the least expensive option. With this option, public access would be restricted to hikers with, possibly, limited access to bicycles and horses. The city said it would cost around $128,000 to maintain and protect the property in its current state. Proponents of this option said they would accept a campground at Sycamore Grove to cover the costs of maintaining the property.[4]

Museum, Bicycles, Horses and a Garden. Central to this mixed-use option was a natural history museum. The Santa Cruz Museum Association had long been looking for a space into which to expand the city museum, currently on a small patch of land in a neighborhood on the east side of Santa Cruz with very little parking. "What better place for a natural history museum than in a setting like this?" asked Robert Stephens, chairman of a museum task force working on plans to develop the museum.[5]

Part of the pitch by the museum was that they would work to promote conservation of Pogonip, to preserve it and to protect and restore its habitats. They already served 12,000 schoolchildren and hoped to expand this number with the "outdoor classroom" offered by Pogonip. They intended the new museum to be enjoyed by children, the disabled, hikers, cyclists, and equestrians, all of whom would understand the message: "Tread lightly on Pogonip."[6]

Of course, there was much to be done: restrooms were needed and adequate parking and the road would need to be upgraded and maintained. And even if a museum was chosen by the task force, the perennial question remained: Could they build a new museum with the classroom and laboratory space they envisioned, or would they run up against the need to preserve the existing clubhouse? The museum advocates said they could build the museum at no cost to the city with private donations, but they needed the City Council's full blessing to help with their fund raising.[7]

The option that supported a museum also opened trails to horses and bicycles as well as to hikers, and advocated a homeless garden. The garden would be a place where homeless people could raise and sell organic produce. It would "provide an opportunity for education regarding human interaction with the environment." They requested only ten acres and claimed they could develop and manage the project using private funding at no cost to the city.

Bicyclists and equestrians were forbidden the use of the network of dirt roads and trails that wound through the Pogonip property. The people who wanted to remove this restriction thought it would improve access to the park as well as provide a link between UC Santa Cruz, other trails in Henry Cowell Redwoods State Park, and

Highway 9. The city said it would require a one-time payment of about $300,000 for signs, trail repair, new trails, and parking. Then it would cost about $82,000 a year to maintain.[8] Proponents claimed, however, that they could maintain the trails at no cost to the city by using volunteers.[9]

Golf and Other Sports. There were many vocal advocates for developing a golf course and playing fields on the Pogonip land. They pointed out that little of Pogonip remained in its natural state due to extensive timber harvesting and cattle grazing in the past.[10]

They claimed that Santa Cruz didn't have nearly enough playing fields and that a city-run golf course would bring money into the city coffers. They claimed a precedent for athletics at Pogonip—the original golf course, the polo fields in the 1930s and 1940s, and the tennis courts of the recent past.

The golf proposal called for a 150-acre course, clubhouse and parking lot. A golf course would be good business for the city.[11] Jim Lang, director of the Parks and Recreation Department, reported that the golf course at DeLaveaga easily paid for itself, "Of all the recreation activities we run, the golf course is the only one that truly pays its own way." Development costs were expected to be around $800,000; fees would cover management costs.[12]

The cost of developing Pogonip

If Santa Cruz decided to develop Pogonip, a 614-acre parcel of open space, what would it cost taxpayers? These are the costs that would be incurred by the city for the various alternatives, according to a task force named to study uses of the property.

Land use	One time development costs	Annual costs	Annual revenues
Hiker, cyclist & equestrian trails and parking	$300,000	$82,000	$0
Homeless/ community garden	Privately funded	Privately maintained	$0
Pogonip Club	Privately funded	Privately maintained	$38,600 lease & taxes
Better access; signs, roads	$350,000-$500,000	$10,000	$45,000 auto entrance fees
Campground	$325,000-$450,000	$65,000	$239,000
Sportsfields	$500,000	$80,000	$0
As is-hikers only	$0	$128,000	$0
Golf course	$7,700,000 (loan could be reimbursed with user fees)	User fees will cover costs	$484,000 - 868,000 user fees

(Chris Carothers ; Source: City of Santa Cruz)

Nevertheless, this remained the most controversial option. Opponents pointed out that the course would require significant grading and would damage vegetation and habitat, fundamentally changing the character of the land. Despite the claims that a golf course would pay for itself eventually, the initial cost was significant.

The question of whether Santa Cruz had enough playing fields was also open to debate. Bruce Kennedy, head of the State Department of Parks and Recreation, claimed there were no definitive studies and argued that cities ended up providing facilities to whichever group made the most noise. "These things are purely political," he said. However, Santa Cruz Recreation Supervisor, Conrad Sudduth, made his own study, which showed no more fields now than there had been twenty years before and about four times as many people playing on these few fields.[13] The city said it would cost $500,000 to develop four sports fields and about $80,000 a year to maintain them.

The Council Decides

The Santa Cruz City Council met to decide the fate of Pogonip on Tuesday evening, January 26, 1993. The meeting was held at the Civic Auditorium and was attended by over 500 people. So many people wanted to speak that the council had to draw lots to determine who could testify. Late that night a majority of the council chose the mixed-use option.

When the vote was finally taken, the council ruled 6 to 1 that Pogonip was "not suitable" for a golf course or for sports fields. Against the wishes of the purists, they voted to allow a museum, a homeless garden, and mixed-use trails. The sole dissenter was Louis Rittenhouse who voted for a golf course and sports fields and who claimed there were other places in the city for a museum.[14]

The Clubhouse Once Again

The Pogonip clubhouse was conspicuous by its absence from the City Council deliberations. In 1992 and 1993 the clubhouse was still leased by the Pogonip Club and was not a concern for the city. At the end of 1993, when the Pogonip Club closed its doors, the clubhouse became the responsibility of the city. Talk began once again. What to do about it? Was it a historic resource or was it an eyesore?

The clubhouse waiting for restoration, its windows boarded up, the weeds grown high, (James M. Morley)

Over the ensuing years there were several flurries of interest. In January of 1995, the City Council held a meeting to review plans for restoring the clubhouse. Only one application was made. Douglas Deitch offered to put up $100,000 of his own money towards restoration of the clubhouse. He planned to start a non-profit corporation and place the clubhouse on the National Register of Historic Places. Deitch had successfully opposed demolition of the clubhouse back in 1991. Now he had plans to restore it and open a new Pogonip Club.[15]

A subcommittee of the Santa Cruz City Council rejected this plan in May. Mainly, they were not interested in private "exclusive" development in Pogonip. In addition, they were concerned that the plan was too vague, that it did not specify all the uses of the property nor where the rest of the money was coming from.[16] In July of 1995, the full council unanimously rejected Deitch's plan. Now they were back to square one: they still had to decide what to do with the clubhouse.

The next year, in June of 1996, the City Council once again formed a task force to discuss other options. Deitch considered this "another dilatory expensive tactic to protract and extend the process of moving forward...." While the task force considered its options, the Parks and Recreation Department sent out crews to "mothball" the clubhouse, essentially to try to preserve it against further degradation. Funding for reconstruction remained the big problem.

The Final Master Plan

In July of 1998, the City of Santa Cruz Parks and Recreation Department issued its "Final Master Plan" for Pogonip. The plan envisioned mixed use of the Pogonip area. Its stated objective was to "Foster appreciation and understanding of the natural environment, as well as human interaction with the environment." Specifically, the plan would:

- Rehabilitate the clubhouse as a meeting and retreat center.
- Create outdoor education facilities in the form of a half-acre day-use outdoor camp in the Sycamore Grove area.
- Enhance existing trails, rerouting trails where needed to protect sensitive areas, and build a mixed-use trail to connect Henry Cowell Redwoods State Park with UC Santa Cruz.
- Provide a permanent garden for the Homeless Garden Project.
- Identify sensitive biotic resources, such as rare plant and wildlife species and unique plant communities.
- Protect and interpret historical structures such as the lime kilns and the McCormick house site.

Some parts of this plan were accomplished. Brochures issued by the Parks and Recreation Department show the location of trails and distinguish between those allowing dogs or horses and bicycles. They also identify historic structures and sensitive biotic areas. In the process, the day-use camp originally planned for the Sycamore Grove riparian area was reassigned to a less biologically sensitive area and Sycamore Grove itself was designated a nature area. The Santa Cruz Museum Association, which had earlier wanted to build a Natural History Museum at Pogonip, had by this time decided to pursue other sites.

At the time this plan was issued, an important addition had been made to Pogonip. In January 1997 the city agreed to purchase from developers the more than 25 acres known as the Wave Crest property for the city's Greenbelt.[17] This property adjoined Pogonip to the south extending to Harvey West Park. This acquisition expanded Pogonip's original 614 acres to 640.

The proposed plan for the clubhouse area of the upper main meadow included a caretaker residence, a new ranger station with a

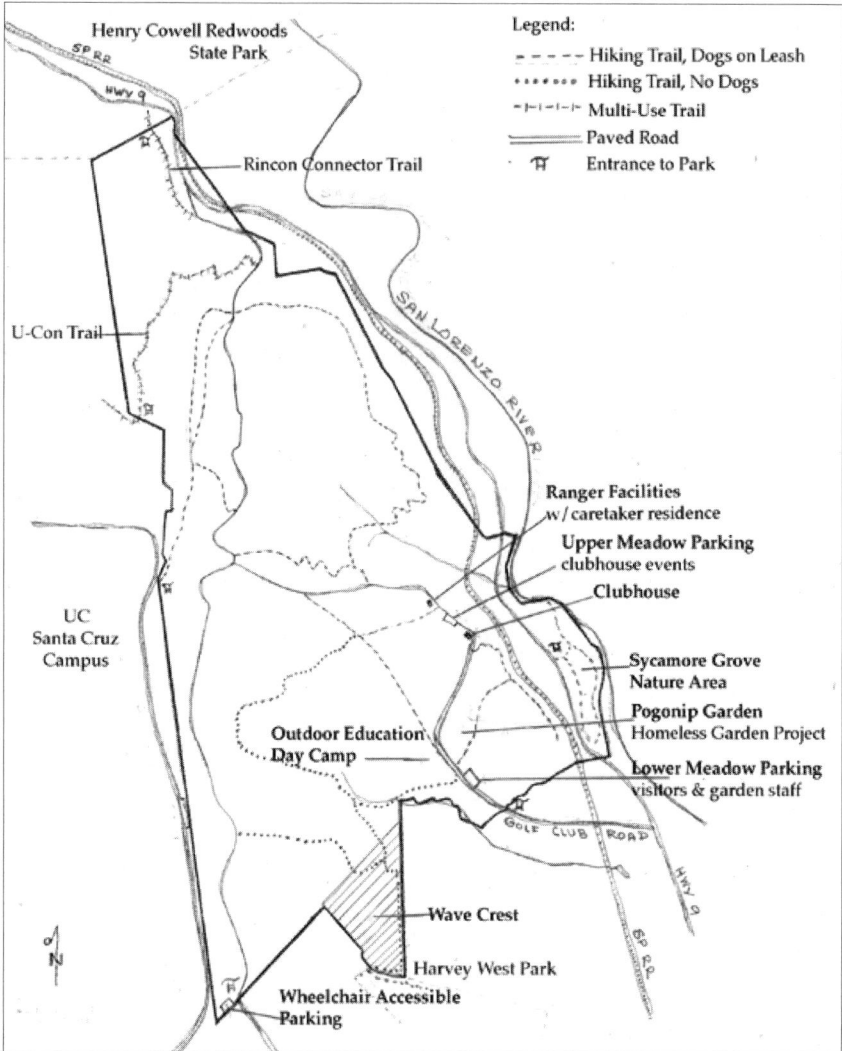

The Parks and Recreation Department vision for Pogonip. Notice that most of the activity is centered in the area adjoining Golf Club Road, leaving the rest of the area preserved for hiking. Only the connector trails in the very north allow bicycles or horses. (Adapted from Santa Cruz City Parks & Recreation Department 1998 Final Master Plan.)

corral for the rangers' horses, and an equestrian training area. An expanded parking lot would replace the tennis courts and there would be a turnaround area for vehicles. All parking and vehicle areas would be screened by shrubbery. Golf Club Road would be

Proposal for the upper main meadow area, showing the parking area, caretaker residence, ranger facilities, and rehabilitated clubhouse. (Adapted from Santa Cruz City Parks & Recreation Department 1998 Final Master Plan.)

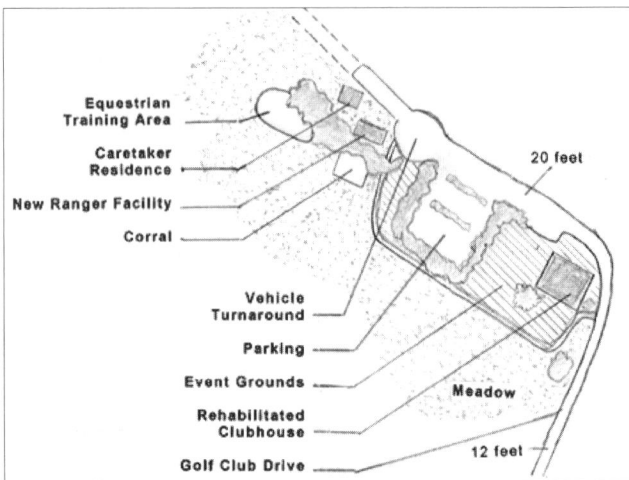

Equestrian Training Area

Caretaker Residence

New Ranger Facility

Corral

Vehicle Turnaround

Parking

Event Grounds

Rehabilitated Clubhouse

Golf Club Drive

20 feet

Meadow

12 feet

widened from its existing ten feet to twelve feet and then to 20 feet where it entered the parking area. The pool would be filled in to provide an area where outdoor special events could take place. And best of all, the clubhouse would be rehabilitated while keeping its historic characteristics, such as "the front porch and façade, the roofline, unique redwood features, main room and stone fireplace, and interior balcony balustrade."[18]

These plans showed what might be accomplished should sufficient funding become available. In the spring of 2000, the city of Santa Cruz was granted the money to hire an architectural firm to draft plans for restoring the Pogonip Clubhouse.[19] In June of 2001, the Pogonip Clubhouse was added to the California Register of Historical Resources.[20] At that time, the city applied to the state for a grant of $500,000 to pay for minimal repairs. By this time, however, total restoration would cost over $2 million. Described as attracting "rats, bats, termites, bees and the occasional vandal," it continued to sit there at the edge of the beautiful meadow, "sagging and rat-infested."[21]

In April of 2001, the California Coastal Conservancy came through with the requested $500,000. However, the city could not use the funds on the clubhouse until it raised the rest of the necessary $2 million.[22] And that could take years. As of this writing, the Pogonip clubhouse still languishes behind its locked chain link fence; the city has all the approvals for its plans to renovate but still lacks the funding.

The City of Santa Cruz waits to unlock the potential of Pogonip and its historic clubhouse.
(Bill Lovejoy)

A Connector Trail

Probably the most visible accomplishment of the 1998 Master Plan was the multi-use connector trail across the top of Pogonip. For a number of years, bicyclists and equestrians had dreamed of a trail that would run through UC Santa Cruz to connect Wilder Ranch State Park with Henry Cowell Redwoods State Park. The problem was that the trail would also have to run through Pogonip. Despite the decision by the City Council in 1993 to allow mixed-use of the Pogonip trails, this question was still not settled four and a half years later in the summer of 1997. At that time the Parks and Recreation Department recommended a "full study on possible impacts" before the council made a decision.[23] As a result, the council allocated $120,000 to pay for an environmental review and a fire-management plan for Pogonip. One concern was where to place a trail that was acceptable to both UC Santa Cruz and Henry Cowell Redwoods State Park.[24]

By September of 1997, a possible connector trail had been mapped out. The trail would be up at the very top of Pogonip. It would start on UC Santa Cruz land, go from Chinquapin Road to Fuel Break Road, turn south to Rincon Trail and then swing north into Henry Cowell Redwoods State Park. Subsequently, the trail was redesigned to meet Rincon Trail well to the north, thereby keeping it at the far northern tip of Pogonip.

After a number of years and a lot of work, on June 19, 1999, the University Connector Trail across Pogonip—shortened to U-Con Trail—was dedicated in a festive ceremony.[25] The half-mile trail had been built over the course of many months by a group of dedicated volunteers from both the Horseman's Association and the Mountain Biker's Association. They worked around delicate habitats, such as

137

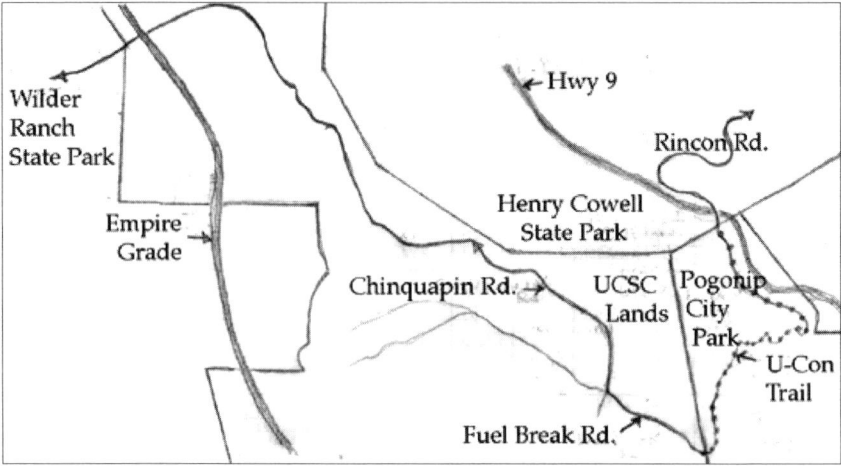

The trail system connecting Henry Cowell Redwoods State Park with Wilder Ranch State Park. The U-Con trail, at the very northern tip of Pogonip, is shown by a dotted line. (From a Santa Cruz County Horseman's Association map, courtesy of Claudia Goodman)

wetlands and avoided steep grades and other hazards. Bud and Emma McCrary were prime movers. Bud McCrary, co-owner of Big Creek Lumber Company had years of trail-building experience. He laid out the trail, then he plowed a four-foot wide track with a backhoe, and finally, volunteers clipped away another four feet of underbrush.[26]

U-Con Trail runs from the university through Pogonip to meet the existing Rincon Trail that connects with Highway 9 at the northeastern edge of Pogonip. Another trail, the Rincon Connector Trail, connects Rincon Trail with a trail in the Henry Cowell Redwoods State Park to the west of Highway 9. Together these trails provide the horse and bicycle connection between the Henry Cowell park and the Wilder park.

Now that the trail was built, most of the maintenance would devolve on the city. Sharon Galligan, supervising park ranger at Henry Cowell Redwoods State Park, anticipated the need for future training so UC Santa Cruz, the city, and state parks could work together to maintain the trail system. "The most important thing," she said, "is that people use the trails safely and responsibly."[27]

The Homeless Garden Project

In 1998, the Homeless Garden Project badly needed a new home. That year, the City Council sold the site of their previous garden on Pelton Avenue. Once again, they looked to Pogonip. At first it did not seem promising. They did not fare well in an earlier draft environmental report on the garden dated April 1998.[28] A few months later at the beginning of July, the Parks and Recreation Commission recommended against giving the garden any space in Pogonip. This was in direct conflict with the Parks and Recreation Department's own recommendation in its Final Master Plan of the same month, as well as with that of the Greenbelt Committee, a three-member subcommittee of the City Council. The Greenbelt Committee had voted to locate the Homeless Garden Project on about 9 acres of Pogonip. Council member Mike Rotkin said, "I don't think a 9-acre garden is an unreasonable amount of use."[29]

To resolve this conflict, the council scheduled a special meeting at the end of July to consider the Homeless Garden Project's request for Pogonip land. At that meeting, Lynne Baseshore Cooper addressed the council:

> In order to provide our service, the Homeless Garden Project has to rely on the certainty of land....For our workers, the certainty and responsiveness of the land is what nurtures their own ability to grow and create and be productive....We have learned that with temporary land our investments are lost and our ability as a project to meet our potential is severely hindered. Ironically, temporary use is the very opposite of sustainable stewardship....I hope that the Council and the community at large can see that our desire for a permanent site at the Pogonip is based on our commitment to serve homeless people in the best way we know how.[30]

On July 21, 1998, the Santa Cruz City Council responded to this plea. They voted to allow the Homeless Garden Project to have a nine-acre plot in the lower meadow of Pogonip below the old clubhouse. Although they couldn't start right in digging up their plot—serious environmental issues had yet to be resolved—they had triumphed over the biggest obstacle: permission to use the land.

In 2003, the environmental impact assessment was completed and the Project began to raise money and look for sources of water.[31] As of 2007, the Project is still waiting to move its garden to Pogonip.

Eastern Access

Throughout their planning for Pogonip, the City of Santa Cruz had not directly addressed the question of an eastern access to UC Santa Cruz. But, it simmered in the background. Residents of the Westside of the city were tired of sitting in gridlock in the early mornings and late afternoons as cars drove to and from the university. Traffic was particularly bad heading from High Street down Storey Street to Mission between two and five in the afternoon. People could sit for as much as 20 minutes. In October of 2003, angry Westside residents gathered more than 1,000 signatures and took their petition to the City Council. They wanted some relief, whether it was a road or a tram or a light rail system.[32]

According to a UC Santa Cruz traffic study, almost half the traffic to the campus passed by Highway 9, where the eastern access route would start. The county grand jury weighed in on the side of an eastern access, recommending that the city reconsider the question of access through Pogonip. At this same time, the city was completing a Master Transportation Study, which was partly financed by the university. However, of its 300 pages, only a page and a half addressed the university-related traffic that had particularly angered Westside residents.

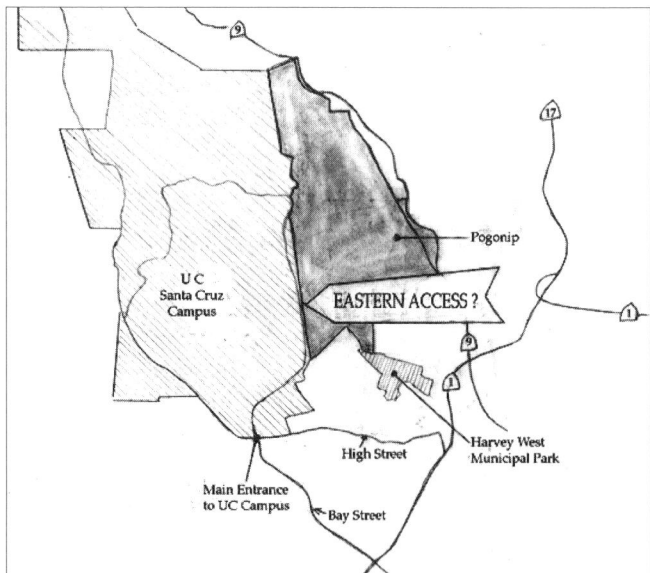

Eastern access to UC Santa Cruz is proposed once again by a citizens group tired of traffic near the university's main entrance.
(Adapted from a Sentinel map)

Referring to the county Grand Jury's recommendation for eastern access, Mike Rotkin called it a "fool's errand." When it came up again before the City Council, he reiterated this opinion. Citing twenty years experience on the council, Rotkin called it a waste of time. In particular, he pointed out that it didn't make sense. He asked, "Where would the traffic go if it didn't run through High Street? It would dump onto Highway 9, a road already snarled by traffic from the San Lorenzo Valley and from businesses in the Harvey West neighborhood." Traffic was a mess there too.[33]

There were other arguments: The university was no longer pushing for eastern access. The original agreement to allow a road through Pogonip had expired in 1999. Shortly after that, as part of an agreement over a disputed parking garage, the university had agreed not to pursue an eastern access.

From the environmental point of view, it would be impossible to develop a road across Pogonip without affecting grasslands or wetlands. Like Lighthouse Field thirty years earlier, this was a "religious" issue. Councilman Scott Kennedy said there was no way a ballot measure would succeed. "Just forget it," he said.[34]

Finally, it was financially untenable. The terrain up to the university was so steep and rugged that a bridge would be required to carry the road. Neither the city nor the university, both facing hard times, had the millions of dollars it would cost to construct an environmentally-friendly access road or light rail line.

It was no surprise when the City Council, at a meeting on December 9, 2003, made a resolute statement: no access road through Pogonip, no way, no how.[35]

A Magnet To Trespassers

Throughout much of Pogonip's recent history it has been a magnet to trespassers. Even when the Pogonip Polo Club leased all 600 acres of the Pogonip land, most of the activity took place in and around the clubhouse leaving the rest of the property open to vagrants. As years passed, the Pogonip Club leased less and less of the land until, in its last days, it leased only the two and a half acres immediately surrounding the clubhouse. The rest of Pogonip was under Cowell Foundation management.

The Cowell Foundation took strong measures to prevent trespassing. They did not allow even day hikers onto the Pogonip land unless they filed a special request. Nature hikes and horseback rides were allowed, but only with proof of insurance and a letter stating the time of use. The Cowell Foundation achieved some success enforcing its rules when, in the 1980s, they hired guards to patrol the land on horseback. This method worked pretty well, but it cost about $40,000 a year. [36]

After the City of Santa Cruz acquired Pogonip in 1989, the problem of trespassing did not go away. Pogonip is now open to day hikers on clearly marked and maintained trails. But, the edges of the grassy main meadow, a number of smaller meadows, hidden areas of open woodland, and streamside nooks provide tempting campsites. People living at these sites sometimes cause serious problems for Pogonip. They may dump their trash, leave campfires unattended, or disturb sensitive habitats.

It is not easy to patrol Pogonip. It is large and its terrain is diverse. It adjoins areas of Santa Cruz with a large homeless population. And with only one ranger to patrol the many parks in the city, it is hard to find and cite all the illegal campers. As a result, off to the side of the main trails, back in the woods, small tents can occasionally be glimpsed. Now, in 2007, three new rangers have been added to the city staff. Let's hope they can protect this open space from further degradation.

Conclusion

The vote to accept the mixed-use option for Pogonip was taken in January 1993, and the final master plan for Pogonip was released in July 1998. In the ensuing years little has been done to implement the plan. As of this writing in 2007, Pogonip is not home to a homeless garden, the Pogonip clubhouse is closed, and trails are still restricted to hikers except for the short multi-use connector trails.

Why is it that the plans for further development of Pogonip have not been implemented? The main reason, of course, is lack of money. Most of these plans could come to fruition if the city had the necessary money. But possibly the answer also lies in the number of people who are satisfied with the status quo—a Pogonip that preserves open space and provides a sanctuary for plants and animals and for the hikers who cherish them.

Chapter Fourteen

Pogonip Today

Pogonip today is a recreation area open to all. Where once it was the site of organized games – golf, polo, and tennis – it is now primarily dedicated to walking, hiking, and running.

Pogonip Trails

Pogonip has approximately eight miles of clearly marked trails. Most of these trails are limited to foot traffic. A short multi-use trail, which connects Henry Cowell Redwoods State Park with Wilder Ranch State Park through Pogonip and the UC Santa Cruz campus, allows horses and bicycles. Many of the hiking trails allow dogs on leash; but dogs are forbidden on the trails devoted to nature.

Sign shelters at the entrances display a large map and provide information about Pogonip, including warnings about how to avoid poison oak, ticks, and mountain lions. The sign shelters at the two main entrances—one at the top of Spring Street, the other where Golf Club Road enters Pogonip—contain a stock of brochures with maps that show the Pogonip trails. Further assistance is provided within Pogonip. Every trail is clearly marked by a wooden post with the trail name and its length in miles.[1]

Topography

The Pogonip map shows trails that seem to meander aimlessly, but that are determined by the topography. Essentially, Pogonip is high and steep on its western border where it adjoins UC Santa Cruz. It descends to lower flatter terrain in the center, and then descends steeply again to the railroad tracks, Highway 9, and the San Lorenzo River on Pogonip's eastern edge.

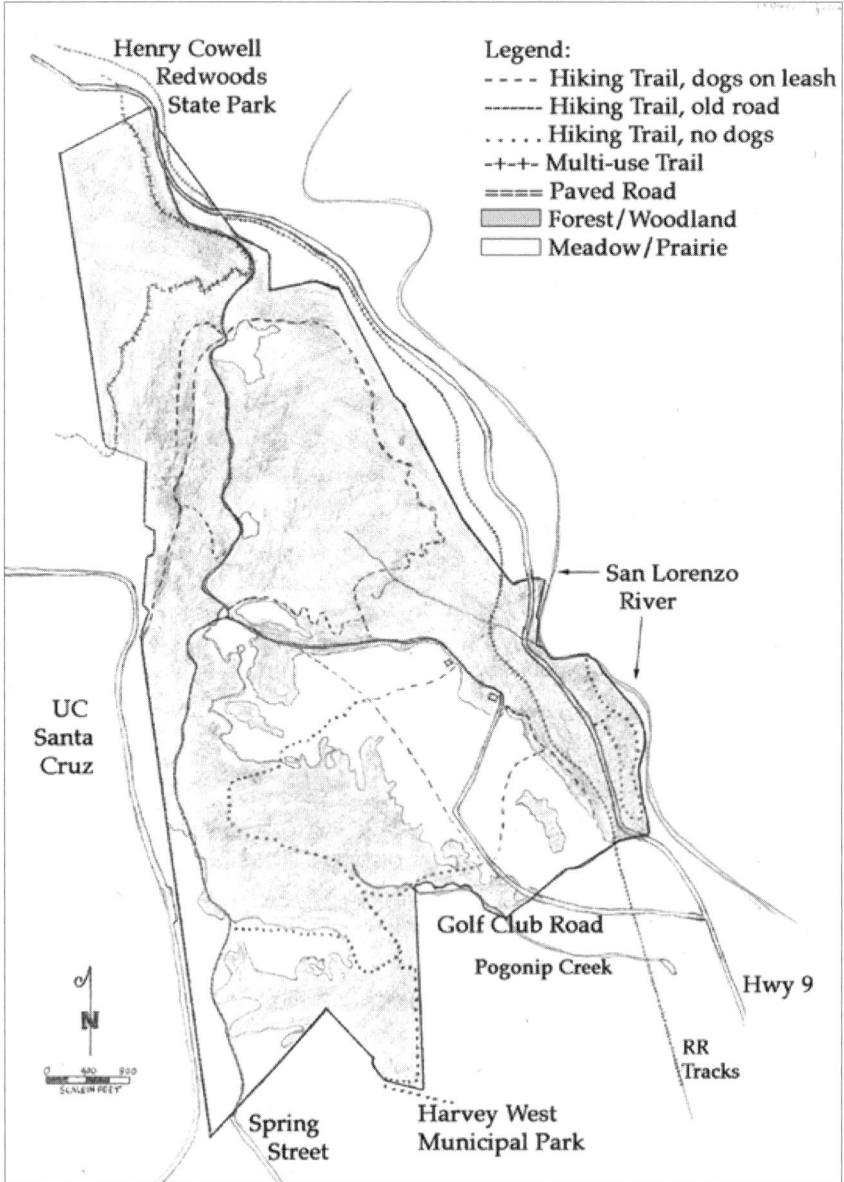

Henry Cowell
Redwoods
State Park

Legend:
- - - - Hiking Trail, dogs on leash
------- Hiking Trail, old road
. . . . . Hiking Trail, no dogs
-+-+- Multi-use Trail
==== Paved Road
Forest/Woodland
Meadow/Prairie

San Lorenzo
River

UC
Santa
Cruz

Golf Club Road

Pogonip Creek

Hwy 9

RR
Tracks

N

0   400   800
SCALE IN FEET

Spring
Street

Harvey West
Municipal Park

From Pogonip's western border with UC Santa Cruz, where the elevation is nearly 600 feet, the land drops steeply to a shelf that parallels that boundary. The old macadam Rincon Road (now labelled Spring Trail and the northern part of the Rincon trail) follows the mostly level contour of this shelf, with elevations varying between 400 and 450 feet. The trails that run east/west, however, have extreme changes in elevation, ranging from highs of 600 feet in the west to lows of 150 feet in the east.

About halfway along the main north/south axis, Brayshaw Trail runs east/west. It almost bisects Pogonip, separating the northern half from the southern half. This trail follows the path of another old road and extends between the Pogonip clubhouse in the east and its intersection with Spring Trail in the west. Forested areas with small meadows lie to the north of Brayshaw Trail; the main meadow lies to its south, gradually descending to Pogonip's southern boundary near the railroad tracks and Highway 9.

The springs that form the headwaters of Redwood Creek and Pogonip Creek lie west of and above the ledge of Spring and Rincon Trails. The creeks themselves run freely in the low-lying riparian areas to the east and south of Pogonip.

Keeping these topographic features in mind should help navigate the Pogonip trails.

Geology

A cursory examination of Pogonip geology provides some further understanding. Along the western edge of Pogonip where it rises up to its boundary with UC Santa Cruz, the metamorphic rocks, schist (sch) and marble (m), predominate. Metamorphic rocks are rocks that have been hardened by heat or pressure, such as marble from limestone and schist from shale. The Pogonip limerock quarries are located at the sites of geologic marble deposits. Limerock is a general term that can apply to either limestone or marble.[2] Deposits of tufa, a porous limestone precipitated from water and rare in the coast range, are found near the springs that rise in this area.[3]

As recently as 1983, geologists found evidence that the Ben Lomond fault extended at least ten miles farther south than previously thought. Extending southeast from its junction with the Zayante-Vergeles fault near Ben Lomond Mountain, the fault runs through Pogonip near its western border where uplift from the fault

145

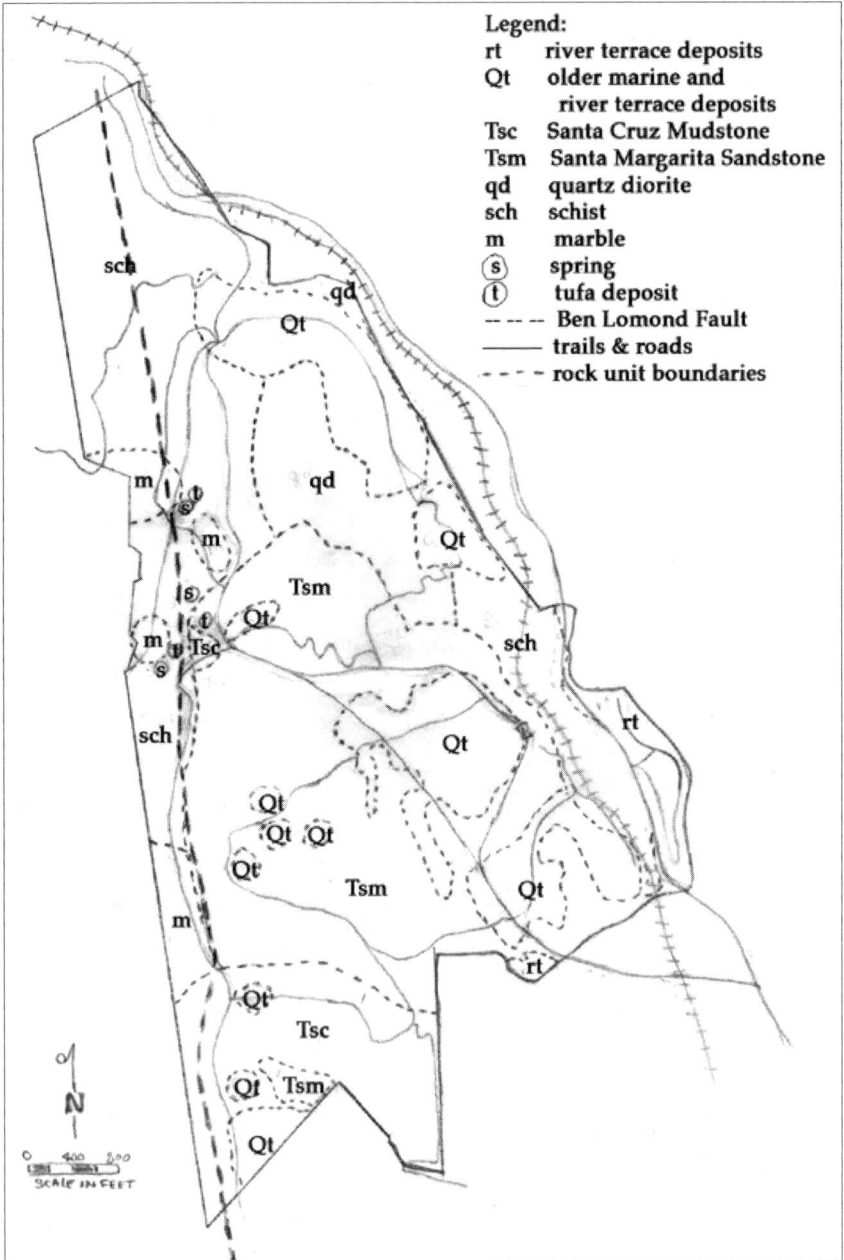

Legend:

rt	river terrace deposits
Qt	older marine and river terrace deposits
Tsc	Santa Cruz Mudstone
Tsm	Santa Margarita Sandstone
qd	quartz diorite
sch	schist
m	marble
ⓢ	spring
ⓣ	tufa deposit
– – –	Ben Lomond Fault
———	trails & roads
– – –	rock unit boundaries

Geologic map of Pogonip. (Adapted from Geologic Map of Santa Cruz County, California, by Earl E. Brabb (1989) and other sources)

has exposed areas of schist and marble. On the east side of the fault are more recent sedimentary deposits, such as Santa Margarita sandstone. The fault is not active; most of the movement on the fault took place about six million years ago.[4]

In the central areas of Pogonip, Santa Margarita sandstone (Tsm) predominates, along with areas of older marine and river terrace deposits (Qt). These marine terrace deposits are found throughout the central area and make up most of the main meadow (where the polo fields and golf course were situated), much of the lower meadow, and some upper meadows. They also occur in small deposits throughout Pogonip.

Quartz diorite (qd), an igneous rock that resembles granite, makes up a portion of the northern part of Pogonip, cropping up through a layer of marine terrace deposits.

At the southwestern tip of Pogonip, along Spring Trail, is an outcrop of Santa Cruz mudstone (Tsc), a siliceous sedimentary rock common to this area. Along Pogonip's eastern edge where it drops down to the railroad and Highway 9, schist predominates, though a small area of quartz diorite is found in its northeast corner. Areas of river terrace (rt) occur in the riparian habitats around Pogonip Creek and Sycamore Grove.[5]

Pogonip creek.
(Don Nielsen)

Ferns and wild iris under an oak canopy. (Don Nielsen)

Habitats

Pogonip contains a wide variety of habitats: open grassland, dark cool forest, and creek beds with riparian growth. A prominent feature of Pogonip is the main meadow. This meadow is mostly non-native grasses, though it contains remnants of old coastal prairie. Most of the rare and unique plant species found at Pogonip are associated with areas of coastal prairie; these include Santa Cruz clover (*Trifolium buckwestorium*) and San Francisco popcorn flower (*Plagiobothrys diffusus*).

The native trees of Pogonip include mixed evergreen forests of coast live oak, tanoak, madrone, and California bay. Upland forests contain Douglas fir and second growth redwoods. Stands of coast live oak also occur within the meadows. Wild iris and California poppies abound on the edges of the meadows. Although it is a retreat of great natural beauty, Pogonip is not a pristine wilderness, having undergone periods of intensive logging.

The chaparral habitat has dense, low-growing thick-leaved plants such as manzanita, huckleberry, sticky monkey flower, coffeeberry, coyote bush, wild mustard and radish. Poison oak is prevalent all through Pogonip.

An area called Sycamore Grove adjoins the San Lorenzo River. It contains California's northernmost stand of central coast cottonwood-sycamore riparian woodland. Other riparian plants occur alongside the creeks that flow through Pogonip and include horsetail, wax myrtle, cottonwood, maple, willow, and ferns.

Wildlife

Bear and antelope no longer roam this area, but an abundance of wildlife remains. Black-tailed jackrabbits, California ground squirrels, Botta's pocket gophers, California voles, and black-tailed deer live in the grasslands and prairie. The smaller mammals provide food for coyote, fox and bobcat as well as raptors, such as the white-tailed kite, great horned owl, and red-tailed hawk. Pogonip is also mountain lion habitat; signs at the entrances warn visitors how to act in the presence of these rarely-seen predators.

Many migratory and resident birds inhabit Pogonip. Birders report seeing western meadowlarks, black phoebes, western bluebirds, American robins, dark-eyed juncos, chestnut-backed chickadees, acorn woodpeckers and sparrows. One year, red crossbills and pine siskins were reported at Pogonip.[6]

Various bat species occupy both the forested areas and the grasslands. Amphibians and reptiles abound; the alligator lizard, western fence lizard, and garter snake are common in the grasslands. The giant Pacific salamander, the California newt, and the banana slug—the mascot of UC Santa Cruz—are all found in the redwood forests. The rare, brilliant green, Ohlone tiger beetle has been observed in the past.

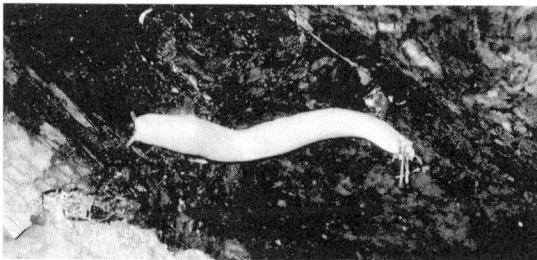

Banana slug (*Ariolimax dolichorphallus*).
(S. Jeanie Taylor)

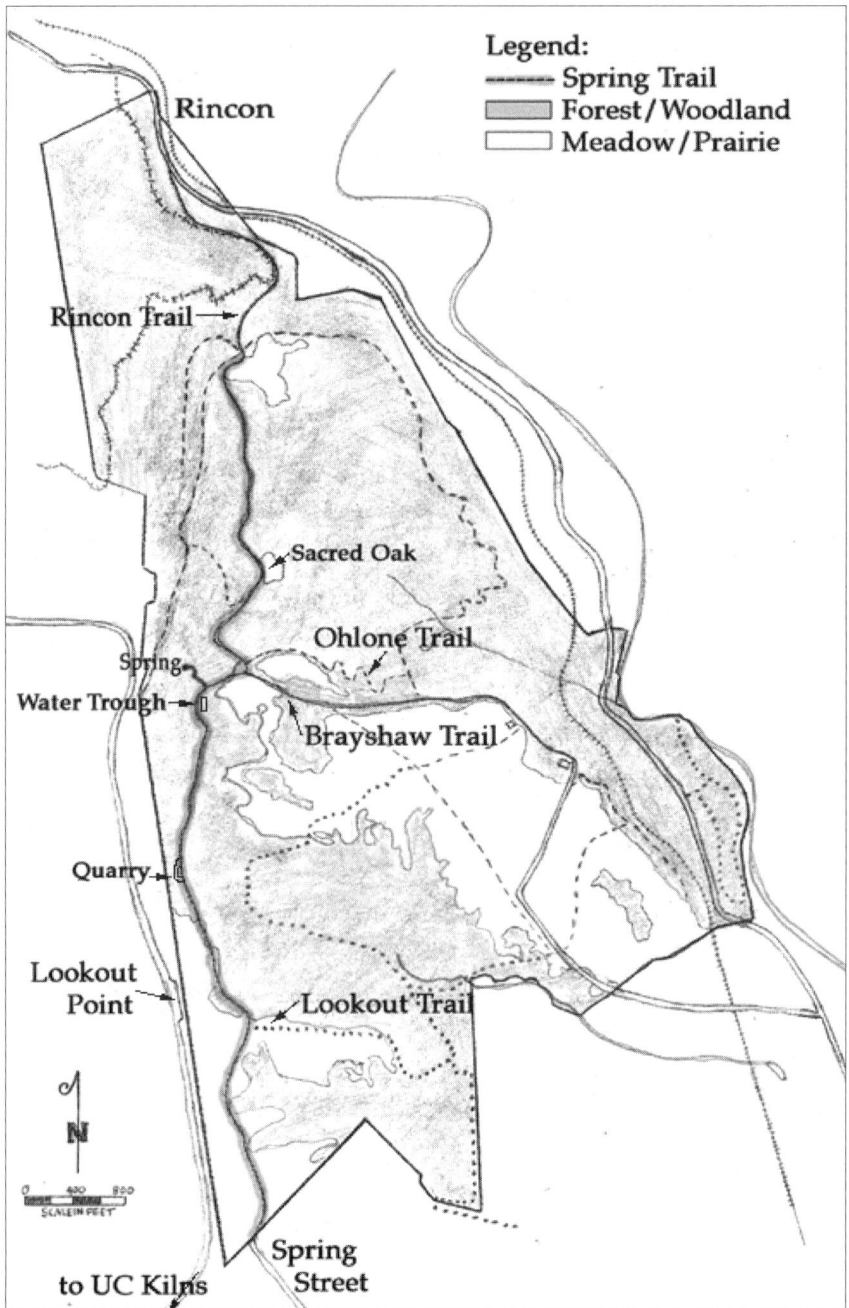

Legend:
------- Spring Trail
Forest / Woodland
Meadow / Prairie

Rincon

Rincon Trail

Sacred Oak

Ohlone Trail

Spring

Water Trough

Brayshaw Trail

Quarry

Lookout
Point

Lookout Trail

N

0   400   800
SCALE IN FEET

to UC Kilns

Spring
Street

Chapter Fifteen

Exploring Pogonip

The history of Pogonip comes vividly to life in the place itself. Exploring the trails through its varied landscape illustrates the importance of Pogonip to Santa Cruz—both to its past and present.[1]

Spring Trail

Spring Trail (1.6 miles) starts at the Spring Street entrance and passes along the western boundary of Pogonip until it meets the Rincon Trail in the north. In its entire length, Spring Trail has little change in elevation.

Spring Trail and the northern part of Rincon Trail together follow the path of the old Rincon Road that once connected the Rincon lime kilns with the kilns at the entrance to what is now the UC Santa Cruz campus. Thus it is a historic resource within Pogonip. It also functions as a service road.

In its southern portion, Spring Trail passes through open meadow dotted with the occasional tanoak and clusters of coast live oak. Coast live oak and tanoak are two of several oaks that produced the acorns used by native Ohlone as a staple of their diet. Tanoak bark provided the tannins once used extensively for tanning leather. The prevalence of tanoaks in this area helped make Santa Cruz the center of California's tanning industry in the late nineteenth and early twentieth centuries.[2] A 1923 map shows the Kron Bros. and Kullman & Salz tanneries located just below the Pogonip area near the junction of Highway 9 and Golf Club Road. Today chemicals are used instead of tanoak bark and the Pogonip tanoaks are no longer logged for their tannin.

Shortly after the Spring Street entrance, Lookout Trail branches off from Spring Trail to the east. This trail is an extension of a trail that once led between Lookout Point, off Coolidge Drive, and

Tanoaks stand out amidst bay and coast live oak just off Spring Trail. (James M. Morley)

Pogonip. This extension to Lookout Trail is now closed, and the entire stretch of meadow between UC Santa Cruz and Spring Trail is off limits to hikers to prevent erosion.

To the west of Spring Trail, before it enters the forested area, is the smaller of the two Pogonip limerock quarries that fed the kilns of the area and provided the base rock used in building nearby roads. Limerock in this area was called "Bluerock" because of its distinctive blue color. The Bluerock and Skeet Club, which once met in the lower meadow below the clubhouse, was probably named for the rock in these local quarries.

After passing through grassland in its southern portion, Spring Trail enters the shade of a forest consisting of second-growth

An old limerock quarry off the Spring Trail, now partially obscured by trees and shrubs. (Joan Gilbert Martin)

Water trough used by oxen or horses in the old days. (Joan Gilbert Martin)

redwoods and mixed evergreens, as well as oaks, bay laurel, hazelnut, bigleaf maple, and alder. At one point the forest opens to reveal a view looking east across the main meadow to the Pogonip clubhouse and the city beyond.

An old cement water trough stands beside the trail in the forested area. It was probably used to water the oxen that transported wood, rock, and lime along Rincon Road in the early days of lime production. The Cowells were known to use ox teams well into the twentieth century long after others had switched first to horses and then to motorized transport.[3]

Immediately across the trail from the water trough at the base of a large redwood tree, the tops of two old metal containers protrude from the ground. These containers still collect water in the winter and were, perhaps, an even earlier source of water for the ox teams.

Just past the water trough, two trails (Brayshaw and Ohlone) branch out to the east, descending steeply to Pogonip's lower meadows and wetlands. Soon, the reason for the name Spring Trail becomes evident. Pogonip Spring, one of several springs in this area, sends a stream across the trail year round. An old spring box and now-broken pipes once provided water to the golf course and polo club that thrived in the meadow below. Above the spring box lie the headwaters of Pogonip Creek. A small forest of bay trees now obscures the view of the main meadow below.

Past the spring, to the east of Spring Trail is a small area of coastal prairie. A path leads down through this meadow to a large oak tree.

The Pogonip
Sacred Oak.
(Paul Lee)

This is the oak that reminded Paul Lee of the image of Christ crucified, as he tells in this story:

> Years ago, I kept a quarter horse at Windy Hill Farm on the top of Spring Street in Santa Cruz. Almost every day I would ride into Pogonip.... One day I rode around an oak tree standing alone in a meadow deep into the park and made it a regular point of destination. And then I noticed it! The downside of the tree was a figure of The Crucified. A limb had been lopped off that left what looked like a head with a semblance of eyes and a mouth and the enormous limbs as outstretched arms. I didn't fall off my horse, like the Apostle Paul was said to have done, but it did make a lasting impression.[4]

Today, the oak is commemorated with this marker at its base:

Coast Live Oak
Quercus Agrifolia
Santa Cruz Heritage Tree
"Pogonip Sacred Oak"
Nominated 1991

Past this spot a number of gushing springs cross the trail. In winter, the area between Spring Trail and the large spring high above it, which feeds Redwood Creek, becomes filled with deep gullies running with water. In this part of the trail most of the forest is second-growth redwood and bay. Spring trail ends at its junction with Rincon and Fern Trails.

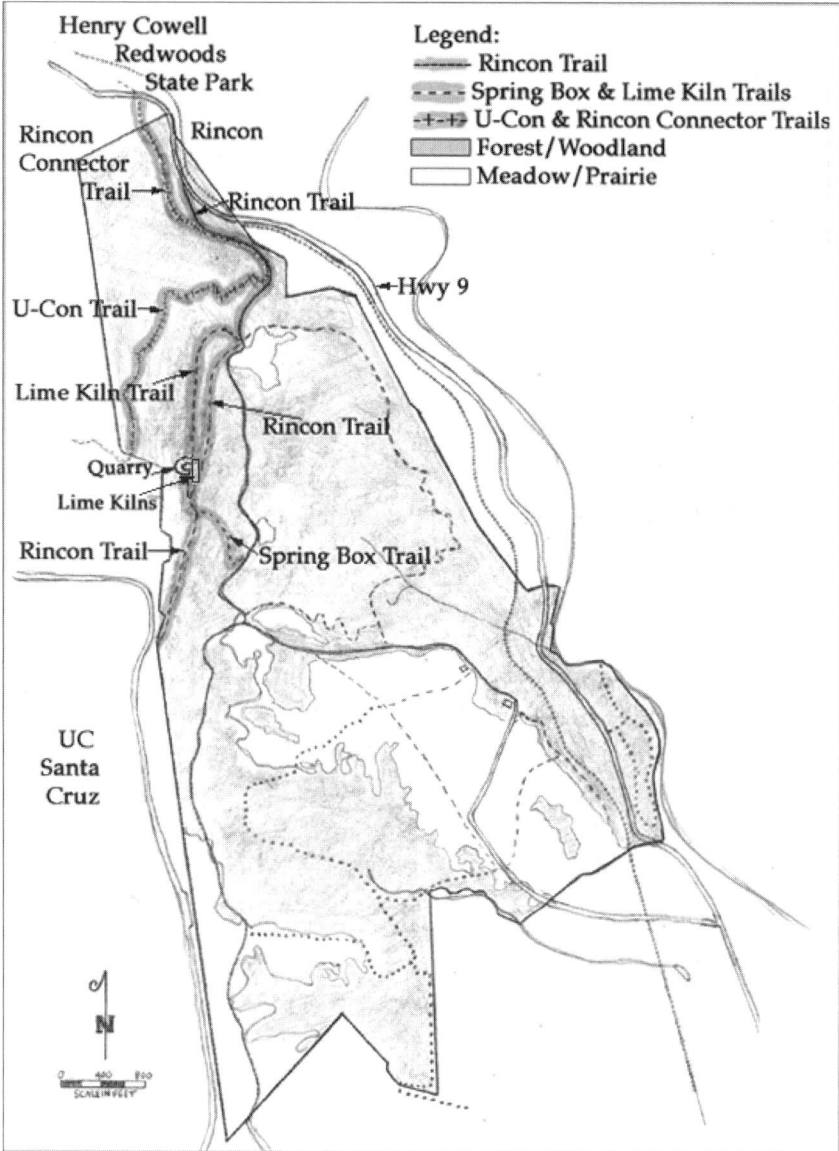

Northern Trails

The densely wooded northern area of Pogonip is located between the UC Santa Cruz campus on the west and Highway 9 on the east with Henry Cowell Redwoods State Park to the north. In this area the trails mostly pass through second-growth redwood. These trails can be entered from Spring Trail, but also from the University campus and from Highway 9.

The very short Spring Box Trail (0.1 miles) starts just past where Pogonip Creek crosses Spring Trail. This trail runs steeply up to the west, passing near a pair of spring boxes in a redwood grove where ferns and moisture abound. The source of the water in the spring boxes is Rincon spring. It rises in the headwaters of Redwood Creek (once called Rincon Creek[5]) and runs down through a small spring box to a larger spring box overflowing with water beneath a towering redwood.

One spring box is now filled with goldfish and a few koi. It wasn't always so. The smaller fish began to appear in the mid 1980s. Perhaps children thought it would be a safe haven for goldfish acquired on a whim. The koi appeared sometime in the early 2000s. Just below the koi pond stands one of the four first-growth redwoods still remaining in Pogonip. It is not a perfectly formed tree—high up its trunk splits to form a second trunk.

Spring Box Trail ends at Rincon Trail. In one direction, Rincon Trail climbs steeply southwest up to the UC Santa Cruz campus. An entrance to this trail off Coolidge Drive provides easy access to hikers from the university. This short steep section of trail is off limits to bicycles and horses, but dogs are allowed on leash. In the other direction, Rincon Trail continues north to Highway 9 where there is an entrance. The entire length of Rincon Trail is 0.9 miles. Teams of horses once pulled loads of limerock down Rincon Trail from what is now the Upper Quarry at UC Santa Cruz to the old Rincon kilns.[6]

Rincon Trail, from its junction with Highway 9 to its junction with Spring Trail, follows the path of the Rincon Road that was used to transport lime and lumber during the last half of the nineteenth and the early years of the twentieth centuries. Spring Trail continues the path of the old Rincon Road south. Local limerock was used to pave these trails and remnants of limerock macadam still show up

Spring box filled with goldfish and a few koi.
(James M. Morley)

The south lime kiln with three arched doorways as it appears today.
(James M. Morley)

on the trails. The limerock helps keep the trails dry through the muddiest winters.

Two old lime kilns stand above Rincon Trail, immediately north of its junction with Spring Box Trail; the south kiln has three doorways, the north kiln has four. The exact history of the Pogonip kilns is not known, though they could be among the oldest kilns in the area.

The lime kilns were used to make lime by heating limerock from local quarries. Fuel was loaded through the doorways at the bottom of the kilns; limerock was loaded from the top. The kilns were built into the hillside, making it simple to load the limerock from above. Each firing required immense quantities of wood. The extensive redwood forests in the area provided this wood and, as a result, the Pogonip forests today consist almost exclusively of second-growth redwood. Only four first-growth redwood trees remain in the entire Pogonip area.

Over time the Pogonip kilns deteriorated. One factor in their deterioration was that redwood trees grew up through them as well as around them. In the summer of 1996, after heated debate, the City Council voted 6 to 1 to remove nine second-growth redwood trees that threatened the kilns. The City has since covered the tops of the kilns with wooden platforms to help prevent further deterioration.[7]

Lime Kiln Trail (0.5 miles) branches off from Rincon Trail just beyond the historic lime kilns. It runs above Rincon Trail past the upper limerock quarry. This large quarry is directly above the lime kilns, which simplified loading the limerock. In the spring, small white and pink Star Flowers bloom along the trail, as well as pink and purple Hounds Tongue. Lime Kiln Trail ends at Rincon Trail. A short distance north of that juncture, Rincon Trail becomes part of the multi-use trail connection.

Multi-Use Trail Connection

The multi-use trail connection was established in 1999. It serves the important function of allowing horses and mountain bicycles (not elsewhere permitted) to cross Pogonip and connect Henry Cowell Redwoods State Park, via UC Santa Cruz, with Wilder State Park. It is made up of three trails. The University Connector or U-Con Trail (0.5 miles) descends steeply from UC Santa Cruz to meet Rincon Trail, which becomes part of the multi-use trail connection for a short distance (0.2 miles). The Rincon Connector Trail (0.2 miles) meets Rincon Trail to provide the northern leg of this system.

An entrance to U-Con Trail lies at the end of Fuel Break Road near the University fire station. A bench at the top of this trail is dedicated to the memory of Chuck Beebe, "Whose persistent efforts enable us to enjoy this beautiful multi-use trail." Chuck Beebe was a member of the Santa Cruz Horseman's Association who "fought like a tiger" to get city permission to build the trail. He also helped design the trail and was instrumental in opening Wilder Ranch as a state park.[8]

A bridge makes a sharp turn to cross a gully on the lower section of the U-Con Trail.
(Joan Gilbert Martin)

158

The U-Con trail is fairly steep (a steady 10% grade) and is deeply rutted. In places it has been shored up with "Turf Blocks" to prevent erosion, and a bridge with a dogleg in the middle has been built to cross a deep ravine. This is a not a trail for beginning bicyclists, particularly heading downhill from UC Santa Cruz; it has sharp turns, many rocks, and passes between deep shade and blinding sun.

The Rincon Trail section of the multi-use connection is wide and fairly level. The Rincon Connector Trail is narrow and has its ups and downs, but is not as steep as the U-Con Trail. The Rincon Connector Trail can be entered from Highway 9 across from a parking lot at the southern end of Henry Cowell Redwoods State Park. Most of the bicyclists on the trail start at this end and head uphill to UC Santa Cruz.

Northern Nature Trails

Fern Trail (0.8 miles) and the shorter Ohlone Trail (0.3 miles) are recent. Unlike the previously discussed trails, these nature trails have little historic significance, but they are important as habitat for rare plant species.

The lovely coastal terrace meadow that lies south of Fern Trail has been called Ghost Meadow, Hidden Meadow, and Haunted Meadow. The current map of Pogonip provided by the Parks and Recreation Department does not name it, possibly to put a stop to the ghost story associated with the meadow. The idea of a ghost in the meadow started soon after students began arriving at UC Santa Cruz in the mid 1960s. Incoming students were told harrowing tales of the accidental death of a young girl on that very spot. Her ghost,

The so-called "Haunted Meadow" at the junction of Spring and Fern Trails.
(Joan Gilbert Martin)

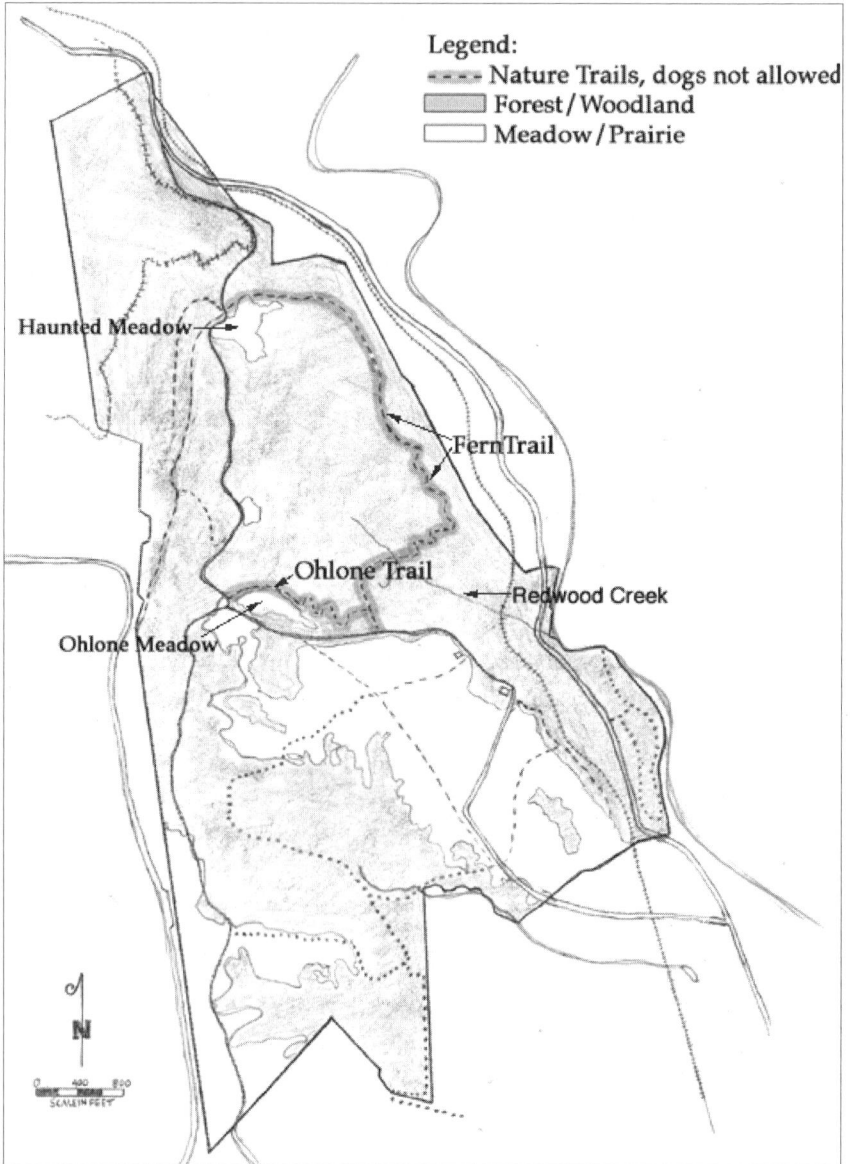

Legend:
- - - - Nature Trails, dogs not allowed
Forest / Woodland
Meadow / Prairie

Haunted Meadow

Fern Trail

Ohlone Trail

Ohlone Meadow

Redwood Creek

N

SCALE IN FEET

dressed all in white, was supposed to appear there on foggy nights.

The local newspapers kept up the story, reporting in a 1975 Halloween article: "Sarah Agnes Cowell, the youngest daughter [of Henry Cowell] was in her late teens on that fateful May morning in 1903 when she took the family buggy and horse from the stable...." The story continues to tell how the horse bolted and how she was thrown from the buggy and killed. It is true that Sarah Cowell was killed in a buggy accident. But she was not killed in this Pogonip meadow. The accident occurred near Cowell's upper kilns in what is now Wilder Ranch State Park. She was not Cowell's youngest daughter, but the second youngest. She was not in her late teens, but was 39 years old when she died on May 14, 1903, only six days short of her 40th birthday.[9]

The woods above the meadow and along Fern Trail are open, consisting mostly of Douglas fir interspersed with bay and madrone. Fern Trail continues along the eastern boundary of Pogonip, gradually descending to cross a bridge over Redwood Creek. Many varieties of fern, including the small five-fingered fern, grow along the creek.

After crossing Redwood Creek, the trail veers west through an area of coastal prairie to meet Ohlone Trail where it turns south to end at Brayshaw Trail. The northern part of Fern Trail once branched off to cross the railroad tracks and Highway 9, providing a link between the main Pogonip area and Sycamore Grove. That portion of the trail is now closed

Ohlone trail rises steeply from the Redwood Creek area. It passes through coastal prairie and other meadowland to end at Spring Trail. Ohlone meadow, south of the trail, is another lovely and isolated meadow. Bracken ferns appear in abundance in the middle of the meadow and along its southern border.

Meadow Trails

The meadow trails consist of: Brayshaw, Prairie, Lower Meadow, and a portion of the Pogonip Creek Nature Loop that traverses the main meadow. Golf Club Road leads from Highway 9 up to the clubhouse. The meadow trails cross a portion of Pogonip that figured prominently in twentieth century Pogonip history. (Spring Trail and the northern trails were important in the last half of the nineteenth and early twentieth centuries.)

The meadow trails traverse the 145 acres where the Casa del

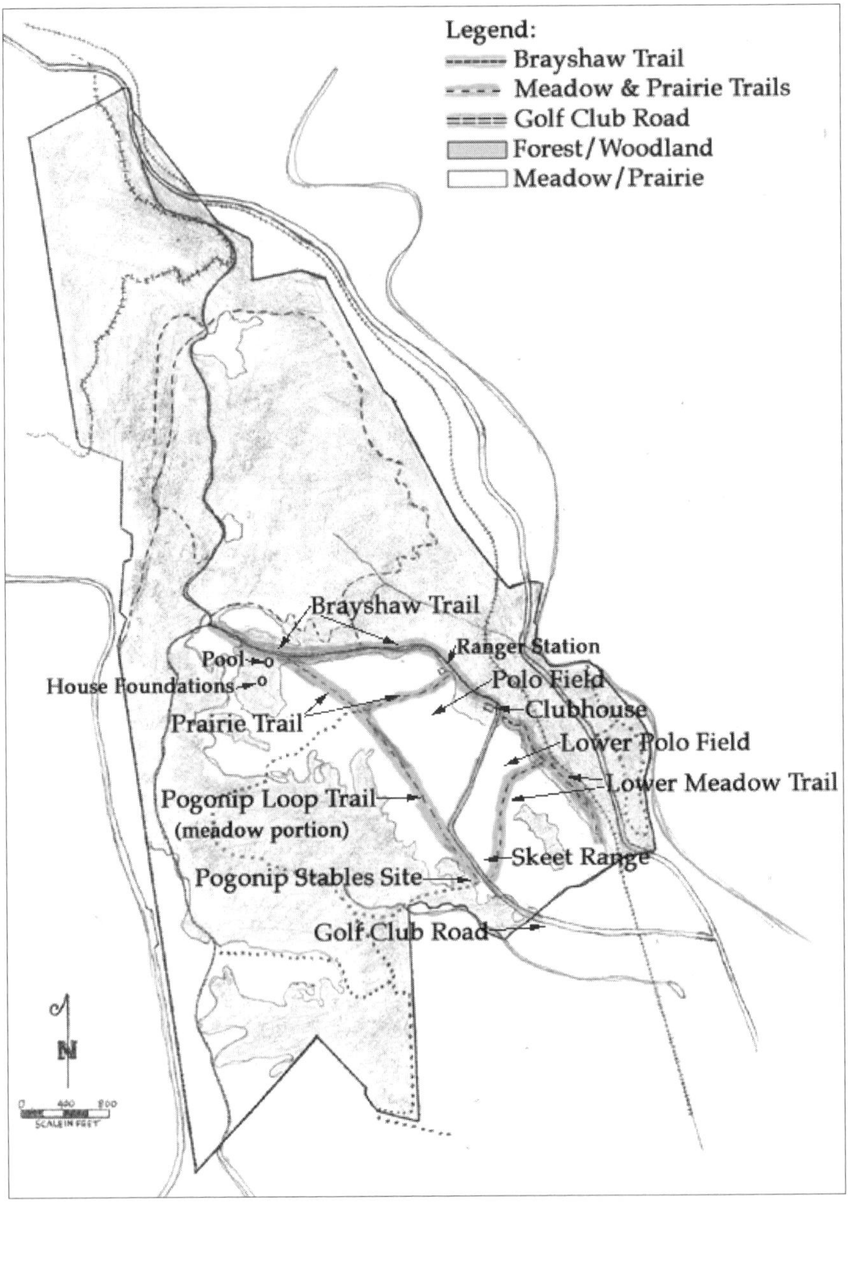
Legend:
Brayshaw Trail
Meadow & Prairie Trails
Golf Club Road
Forest/Woodland
Meadow/Prairie
Brayshaw Trail
Ranger Station
Pool
House Foundations
Polo Field
Clubhouse
Prairie Trail
Lower Polo Field
Lower Meadow Trail
Pogonip Loop Trail
(meadow portion)
Skeet Range
Pogonip Stables Site
Golf Club Road
N
SCALE IN FEET

Rey Country Club, later the Santa Cruz Golf Club, had an 18-hole golf course between 1912 and 1934. They pass near the foundations of the summer mansion built by E. O. McCormick in 1912. They skirt the polo fields used by the Pogonip Polo Club between 1936 and 1948. They pass by the clubhouse of the very social Pogonip Club that thrived between 1948 and 1993. The clubhouse is still standing—a dilapidated reminder of seventy-five years of fun and festivities that started in February of 1912 and continued until February of 1987 when the building was condemned.

Starting at Highway 9, Golf Club Road passes under a railroad trestle to enter Pogonip just past an organic farm. The road has had several names in its time. Oddly, it was called Pogonip Avenue when it led to the golf club and Golf Club Drive when it led to the Pogonip Club.[10] Today, after a series of county name changes following the 1989 earthquake, it is called Golf Club Road. The road is the only paved road in Pogonip. It climbs slowly from the entrance for about two-thirds of a mile to the clubhouse.

The clubhouse is now surrounded by a chain-link fence, as are the weedy and overgrown tennis courts. The tiled edges of the swimming pool can still be seen, but the pool itself is filled with dirt. The terrace in front of the clubhouse, where lunch was once served adjoins the grassy lawn that was once a putting green for the golf club. At the far edge of this lawn stands the redwood grove beloved of Dorothy Deming Wheeler, founder of the Pogonip Polo Club.

Brayshaw Trail (0.5 miles) starts at the clubhouse, goes north past the ranger station, and then veers west to end at Spring Trail. The trail was probably named for Shawn Alan Brayshaw, a young ranger for the Parks & Recreation Department, who died in

The grove of trees at Pogonip where a plaque memorializes Dorothy Deming Wheeler, doyen of the Pogonip Polo Club.
(James M. Morley)

163

December of 1990.[11] On the Parks & Recreation Department map from the early 1990s, the trail was called Gumby Trail; on later maps it has been renamed Brayshaw Trail. For most of its length, Brayshaw Trail is wide and fairly level, meandering gently through both open woodland and meadow. At its western end it rises very steeply (a 25% grade) before meeting Spring Trail. Brayshaw trail, like Spring Trail and the northern end of Rincon Trail, is used as a service road.

A corral once adjoined the ranger station for the horses kept by Pogonip rangers. The horses grazed freely at Pogonip throughout the 1980s—a short scene in the 1987 movie *The Lost Boys* shows horses running wildly across the old polo field. During the 1989 earthquake several of these horses panicked and got loose, ending up in Capitola where they ran up Bay Avenue onto Highway 1. There, one of the horses collided with a car, crashed through the windshield, and killed the driver. His survivors successfully sued the City of Santa Cruz, claiming the horses were not properly fenced.[12] After this tragic event, horses no longer grazed at Pogonip.

Horses were not the only animals once kept on this property. Around 1925 Harry Cowell imported a herd of elk to graze at Pogonip. He also brought in buffalo and Bobwhite quail. He had hoped to establish a conservation area but was unsuccessful. Hunters wiped out the quail and the elk, and the buffalo died of disease.[13] From about 1957 to 1969, local rancher Norman Gotti grazed his cattle at Pogonip, leasing pastureland from the Cowell Foundation.[14]

In 1912, the same year that the Casa del Rey Country Club opened its golf course, club member Ernest O. McCormick leased some land from Cowell and built a vacation estate overlooking the links.[15] He built a large white house with extensive tropical gardens. A pool, which may have served as a reservoir, was built above the house. The house was just south of what is now Brayshaw Trail, which was then an unpaved road that could be traversed by cars. The house appears in photos of both golfers and polo players (see Chapters Three and Six).

McCormick died in 1923, though his family continued to use the estate for a number of years after his death. Later a widow, Mrs. Kate Remington, with her sons, Charles and Walter, lived there. She and her sons, one of whom was developmentally disabled, arrived in 1948 and continued to live at the estate until 1959. The house was abandoned during the 1960s and eventually burned down in the winter of 1974.[16]

Off to the side of the trail leading through the Main Meadow, lies an old rusted mower. Colleen McInerney-Meagher recalls pulling this mower behind a tractor to mow the Pogonip polo field.
(Joan Gilbert Martin)

The pool, now surrounded by a chain link fence, is empty of water except after heavy rains. A tall palm tree stands by the pool as a reminder of the once extensive tropical gardens. Little evidence remains of the house itself, only a low stone wall with steps leading from the house to its gardens and the remains of a pair of stone pillars that once stood at the entrance to the estate.

Prairie Trail (0.3 miles) runs south of Brayshaw Trail, starting near the ranger station and ending near the McCormick house foundations.

The meadow section of the Pogonip Creek Nature Loop (about 0.4 miles) extends between Prairie Trail and Golf Club Road. Dogs on leash are allowed in this section of the loop. It leads across the extensive main meadow, one of the loveliest features of the Pogonip open space. It was this meadow, with its rolling terrain and frequent gullies that made the golf links here some of the best in the region. The eastern edge of the meadow is where the Pogonip Polo Club had its world-class polo field.

The portion of the Pogonip Creek Nature Loop that runs through the main meadow was once called the Old Stables Trail because it led to the Pogonip stables. Deming Wheeler built the stables in 1935 or 1936. (They were not designed, as some have surmised, by William Wurster). The two main buildings held the string of Pogonip polo ponies; there were at one time three or four additional outbuildings. In 1986, these buildings were all collapsed or collapsing—a tree had fallen on one stable—and the Cowell Foundation decided the stables were a danger and had to be demolished.[17]

In the days when polo was played here, a corral and a small

The Pogonip stables in their declining years. (In the foreground, Golf Club Road continues left up to the clubhouse.) The mound in front of the stable at the left is a collapsed shed now covered in vegetation. The remains of the tree that fell on one of the stables is still there. (Debra Morstein Sloss)

training ring for the polo ponies were located just south of the stables. The City of Santa Cruz now has plans for an outdoor education day camp at this spot. The stable trail ends at a gate opening to Golf Club Road.

Across Golf Club Road is another gate leading to Lower Meadow Trail (0.6 miles). Past this gate and north of the trail is where the Bluerock and Skeet Club held its skeet shooting practice and meets. The trail passes through the future site of the Pogonip Homeless Garden and provides an alternate route up to the old clubhouse.

Lower Meadow Trail goes straight across the lower meadow to a line of trees that border the tracks of the Southern Pacific railroad. At that point the trail turns to run south to Pogonip's border and north up to the clubhouse. Along this portion of the trail a smooth flat area was once the practice polo field for the Pogonip Polo Club.

Looking down from the top of Golf Club Road to the lower meadow, with the spire of Holy Cross Church in the distance, right. The smooth area at the left is the lower polo field once used for practice. (Joan Gilbert Martin)

Southern Nature Trails

The biologically sensitive Pogonip Creek Nature Loop can be entered from Lookout Trail, from Golf Club Road, or from Harvey West Trail. Both Lookout and Harvey West Trails forbid dogs, who might disturb the sensitive areas around and above Pogonip Creek. Part of the loop runs down across the main meadow (previously discussed with Meadow Trails; see page 16); this part does not run through a sensitive area and dogs are allowed on leash.

Sycamore Grove, a biologically sensitive area where dogs are not allowed, is separated from the rest of Pogonip by both the tracks of the Southern Pacific railroad and Highway 9.

One way to enjoy the southern nature trails is to return to Spring Trail. Near its beginning, Lookout Trail (0.5 miles) branches off toward the Pogonip Creek area. From an upper plateau with an elevation of around 450 feet, Lookout Trail passes through coastal prairie grasslands and into a mixed evergreen forest and then winds steeply down to an elevation of less than 200 feet.

Along the way, Lookout Trail passes by two of the four first-growth redwoods that remain in Pogonip. One has a broken top and is not as spectacular as the first-growth redwood on the Pogonip

167

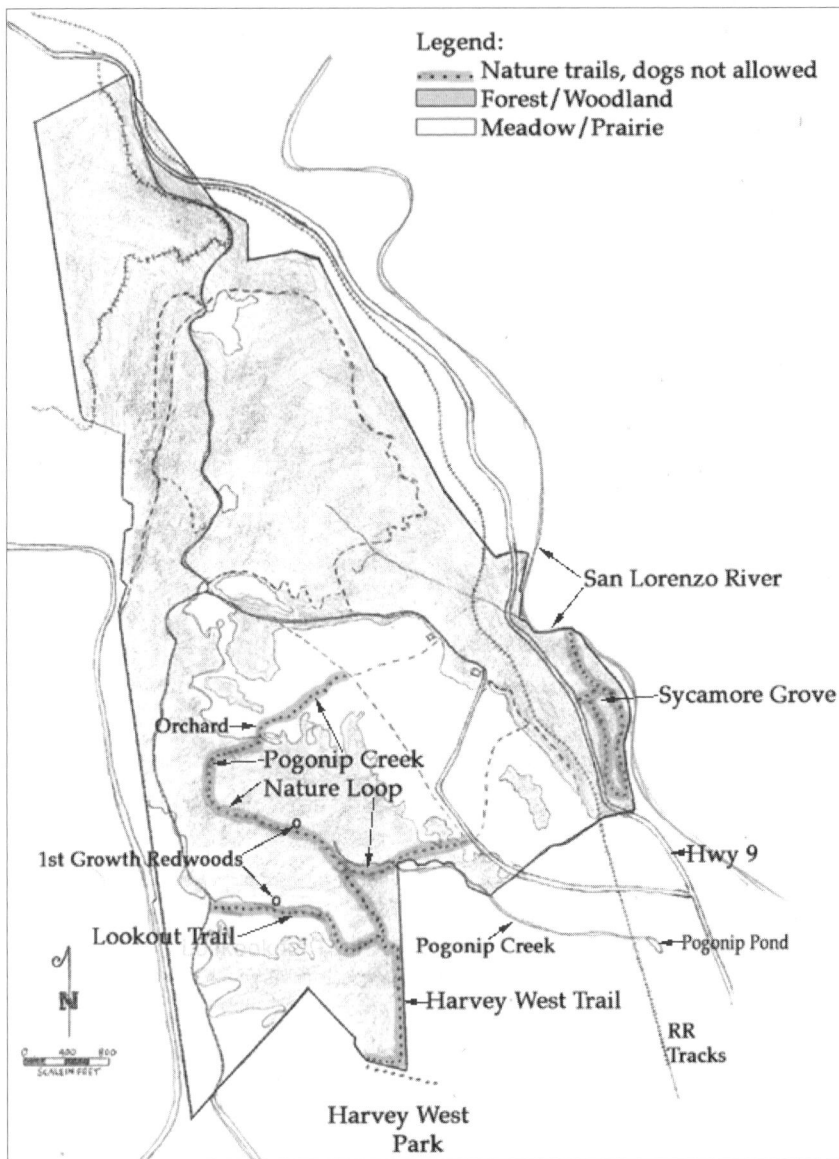

Legend:
..... Nature trails, dogs not allowed
▨ Forest / Woodland
▢ Meadow / Prairie

San Lorenzo River

Sycamore Grove

Orchard→

─Pogonip Creek
Nature Loop

1st Growth Redwoods

Hwy 9

Lookout Trail

Pogonip Creek

Pogonip Pond

N

←Harvey West Trail

RR
Tracks

Harvey West
Park

Loop Trail. After passing these trees, the trail drops down to meet Harvey West Trail, which turns right to make a steep descent to the south, emerging at the top of Harvey West Boulevard.

At the junction of Harvey West Trail, Lookout Trail turns northwest to enter the Pogonip Creek Nature Loop (1.2 miles). This loop trail passes through a wide diversity of plant communities, including coastal prairie,

Two of the first-growth redwoods in Pogonip are just north of Lookout Trail; one redwood is truncated at the top. (James M. Morley)

mixed evergreen forest, central coast riparian scrub, redwood stands, and a bay grove. One can continue north on the loop or turn east to cross Pogonip Creek. Pogonip Creek has its headwaters above Spring Trail and runs year round through the lower part of Pogonip, draining into a pond on private property. From there, it flows in underground pipes to the San Lorenzo River.

After crossing Pogonip Creek on a wooden bridge built by the City of Santa Cruz, the trail runs through an area of Central Coast riparian scrub. Looking down to the south from this trail one can see the industrial area of Santa Cruz adjoining Harvey West Park. The contrast between the peace of Pogonip and the harsh cityscape below is notable. The trail continues to the old stable site near the gate at Golf Club Road. This portion of the trail was once the path taken by riders coming from Windy Hill Farm to Pogonip to play polo. At the gate the loop trail turns north through the main meadow to its junction with Prairie Trail.

Instead of taking the trail across Pogonip Creek, one can continue north on the Nature Loop, passing through a forest of second-growth redwood. The largest and only undamaged first-growth redwood in Pogonip stands to the east of the trail. Climbing out of the redwood forest, the trail passes through a more open wooded area with bays and scrub oaks and then comes out onto a high prairie. Turning and looking back at this point one can see the first-growth redwood standing tall above the surrounding trees.

The trail continues through an old orchard that was once part of the McCormick estate. Two persimmon trees, a walnut and two apple trees still bear fruit. Past the orchard, the nature loop turns east to join Prairie Trail. Midway along Prairie Trail, the loop turns south to run down through the main meadow to the stable site .

Sycamore Grove was once the site of a summer resort; today it is one of the sensitive biotic areas within Pogonip. Situated in the flood plain of the San Lorenzo River, it has the northernmost stand of Central Coast cottonwood-sycamore riparian forest in California. The grove is approximately ten acres and features sycamore, black cottonwood, and various species of willow.[18]

Several sensitive wildlife species including the California red-legged frog and the southwestern pond turtle have been found to the north and south of this grove. Thus, it is possible that the grove is also a habitat for these species. It might also be home to the yellow warbler. In addition, it is a migration corridor and provides valuable nesting and foraging habitat for many common wildlife species.[19]

The only access to Sycamore Grove, at this time, is off Highway 9. The entrance is on the east side of the highway, a half mile from Golf Club Road and before the entrance to Paradise Park. A sign shelter marks the entrance and a pullout provides parking.

Unfortunately, invasive non-native growth has overrun much of the native habitat. Vines, pampas grass, French broom, and acacia trees are only some of the plants that led to this degradation. These non-native plants are largely the result of disturbance when Sycamore Grove Camp flourished here for forty years between 1921 and the early 1960s. Currently, transient camping has brought more trampling as well as trash and debris. The City of Santa Cruz had plans to implement a long-term management program to restore the health and insure the survival of this unique area.

An old stone wall that once marked the entrance to Sycamore Grove Camp.
(Joan Gilbert Martin)

Epilogue

Pogonip's Future

Afternoon on a Hill

I will be the gladdest thing
  Under the sun!
I will touch a hundred flowers
  And not pick one.

I will look at cliffs and clouds
  With quiet eyes,
Watch the wind bow down the grass,
  And the grass rise.

And when lights begin to show
  Up from the town,
I will mark which must be mine,
  And then start down!

Edna St. Vincent Millay

The Pogonip clubhouse will be 100 years old in 2012. At that time it is likely that the grand dame will still be the centerpiece of the 640 acres of natural beauty that surround it. The City of Santa Cruz developed a draft master plan for Pogonip in July of 1998, but nine years later the vision is still only partially fulfilled.

The draft called for rehabilitating the historic clubhouse. It would be used as a staging area for special events, for educational opportunities, including historic interpretations, and possibly as a retreat. Some grant money is available, but further efforts are needed to target interested donors.

As of this writing, a multi-use connector trail has been built that allows horsemen and mountain bikers to cross Pogonip, joining UC Santa Cruz with Henry Cowell Redwood State Park. Environmental and sensitive areas are being protected, and existing trails improved. Much is being done, but much more is needed to make the master plan a reality. A permanent organic homeless garden is yet to be set up in the lower main meadow; this will probably occur when water issues are resolved. An outdoors-camp facility is yet to be established for young people.

Like any living thing, Pogonip must change with changing times. The community of Santa Cruz has inherited a precious resource and only with respect and care by those entrusted with its management can it be preserved.

Notes

Prologue – The Name

1 Donald Thomas Clark, *Santa Cruz County Place Names*, (Santa Cruz: Santa Cruz Historical Society, 1986), p. 260; quote is from Frederick Webb Hodge, ed. *Handbook of American Indians, North of Mexico*, (Washington, D. C.: Bureau of American Ethnology, 1907), p. 272; and *Random House Dictionary of the English Language*, New York, 1966; quoted by Clark.

2 Alfred Doten, *Journals*, 3 volumes 1849-1903, Special Collections, University of Nevada, Reno. Quote is from entry of Sunday, January 8, 1888. He also mentions "pogonip" fog in an earlier entry dated January 21, 1877.

3 Robert E. Burton, "In Search of Santa Cruz—Historic Pogonip Creek Now Harnessed For Lawns, Polo Fields," *Evening News*, October 23, 1938 (Dorothy Deming Wheeler scrapbooks, Special Collections, University Library, UC Santa Cruz.)

4 Donald Thomas Clark, *Santa Cruz County Place Names*, p. 260; quote is from the *Frontier Gazette*, Spring 1959, p. 1.

5 Ibid, p. 260.

6 William Shipley, "The Awáswas Language," *A Gathering of Voices; the Native Peoples of the Central California Coast*, Santa Cruz County History Journal, no. 5, (Santa Cruz: Museum of Art & History, 2002), p. 173.

7 "Seeing through the fog – Unraveling the mystery of poconip [sic]," Douglas Dunaway, Mono Lake Newsletter, Spring 2006, pp. 16, 18. The article discusses the icy fog that forms in the Mono Lake Basin and is known as "poconip;" it also discusses the same fog called "pogonip" in the northern valleys of the Great Basin, particularly in Nevada.

8 "Local Brevities," *Sentinel*, December 4, 1875, p. 3.

9 McHugh Scrapbooks, (Special Collections, University Library, UC Santa Cruz), p. 103. A photo of the cart house is reprinted in an article by Ernest Otto, "Santa Cruz Yesterdays," *Sentinel*, October 26, 1952, p. 6

10 Map of the City of Santa Cruz in 1923, published by Arnold M. Baldwin, Map Library, UC Santa Cruz; and map of Pogonip issued by the Santa Cruz Parks & Recreation Department, undated but prior to 1993, on which the name Salz Pond is written in pencil. (Colleen McInerney-Meagher collection)

11 What Burton calls Big Tree road is now Highway 9.

12 Robert E. Burton, "In Search of Santa Cruz...."

Chapter One – Native Peoples

1 Randall Milliken, "The Spanish Contact & Mission Period Indians of the Santa Cruz-Monterey Bay Region," *A Gathering of Voices*, pp. 25-26.

2 Alfred L. Kroeber, *Handbook of Indians of California*, (New York: Dover Publications, 1976), p. 464.

3 Malcolm Margolin, *The Ohlone Way, Indian life in the San Francisco-Monterey Bay Area*, (Berkeley, California: Heyday Books, 1978), pp. 41-42.

4 Conversations with Robert Edwards and Allan Lönnberg of the Cabrillo College Department of Anthropology; June 8, 2006.

5 Randall Milliken, "The Spanish Contact & Mission Period Indians, p. 27.

6 Malcolm Margolin, *The Ohlone Way*, pp. 62-63.

7 Randall Milliken, "The Spanish Contact & Mission Period Indians, pp. 28-29.

8 Ibid, p. 30.

Chapter Two – The Early Years

1 http://www.learncalifornia.org/ viewed February 2006.
2 Donald Thomas Clark, *Santa Cruz County Place Names*, pp. 276-277.
3 "California's Pioneer Wine Families," *California Historical Society Quarterly*, vol. 54, pp. 140-141.
4 Suñol had come to California from Spain, possibly as early as 1818, and married into the Bernal family. Around 1839, he was granted the Rancho Valle del San Jose, a vast tract of almost five thousand acres. His son, Jose Narciso Suñol settled in the Suñol Valley. *History of Alameda County, California,* (Oakland: M. W. Wood, 1883), p. 983.
5 Hubert Howe Bancroft, *History of California*, (San Francisco: A. L. Bancroft, 1884-90) vol. 4, p. 685; vol. 5, 660; and vol. 5, p. 641.
6 Leon Rowland Card Files, box B-1, card 161 (Special Collections, University Library, UC Santa Cruz).
7 Leon Rowland Card Files, box B-3, cards 239, 240, 276, and 289.
8 Hubert Howe Bancroft, *Register of Pioneer Inhabitants of California, 1542-1848, and index to information concerning them in Bancroft's History of California, volumes I –V,* (Los Angeles: Dawson's Book Shop, 1964) R-Z, pp. 708-709; R-Z, p. 738; and Leon Rowland Card Files, box A-6, card 271.
9 Edward Martin, *History of Santa Cruz County, California with Biographical Sketches...* (Los Angeles: Historic Record Company, 1911), p. 314.
10 Susan Lehmann, *Fully Developed Context Statement for the City of Santa Cruz,* (Santa Cruz: City of Santa Cruz Planning & Community Development Department, 2000), p. 9.
11 Edward Martin, *History of Santa Cruz County, with Biographical Sketches,* p. 314.
12 Kenneth Jensen, "The lime industry in Santa Cruz County," unpublished manuscript, Special Collections, UC Santa Cruz, 1976, p. 6; and Clinton E. Fehliman, "Economic history of Santa Cruz County, California, 1850-1947," unpublished manuscript, Special Collections, UC Santa Cruz, 1947, p. 30.
13 Frank Perry, et al. *Lime Kiln Legacies,* (Santa Cruz: Museum of Art & History, 2007), pp. 60-61; Supreme Court of the United States. *The California Powder Works; plaintiff in error vs. Willis Davis, Administrator of estate of Isaac E. Davis and Henry Cowell.* Record Case No 14,346, October Term # 1893, Term No. 301, pp. 230-233.
14 "Our Town," *Sentinel,* February 21, 1861, p. 2; and "Improvements in Santa Cruz," *Sentinel,* April 18, 1861, p. 2
15 "New Saw-Mill," *Sentinel,* July 4, 1862, p. 2.
16 "The work has not been stopped...," *Sentinel,* December 1, 1866, p. 3. The article refers to a road that runs along the Davis and Cowell road, presumably the Rincon Road.
17 Frank A. Perry, et al., *Lime Kiln Legacies,* p. 152.
18 *Ibid.*
19 Frank A. Perry, et al., *Lime Kiln Legacies,* p. 160.
20 "Death of a Santa Cruz Pioneer," *Sentinel,* November 24, 1866, p. 2; and "Schooner A. P. Jordan," *Sentinel,* February 2, 1867, p. 2.
21 "Sold," *Sentinel,* July 15, 1965, p. 3; and Leon Rowland Card Files, box A-2, card 464, Special Collections, University Library, UC Santa Cruz. Both sources report that Cowell paid $100,000 for Jordan's share. Other sources indicate that the transaction was more complicated, including two of Jordan's ships.
22 Laurie MacDougall, *Henry Cowell and His Family (1819—1955): A Brief History,* (San Francisco: S. H. Cowell Foundation, 1989), p. 11.
23 Josephine McCracken, "The Home of the Cowells," Overland Monthly, July 1912, pp. 17-23.
24 Leon Rowland Card Files, box A-2, card 464. The cost was reportedly $400,000.
25 George Cardiff, *Santa Cruz and the Cowell Ranch, 1890-1964,* an interview by Elizabeth Spedding Calciano, (Santa Cruz: University Library, UC Santa Cruz, 1965), p. 188.
26 Ernest Otto, "Santa Cruz Yesterdays," McHugh Scrapbooks, Vol 1, Special Collections,

University Library, UC Santa Cruz.

27 George Cardiff, *Santa Cruz and the Cowell Ranch, 1890-1964*, pp. 169-170.

28 Robert W. Piwarzyk and Michael E. Miller, *Valley of Redwoods, A Guide to the Henry Cowell Redwoods State Park* (Felton, California: Mountain Parks Foundation, 2006), p. 37
A portion of Henry Cowell Redwoods State Park was formerly Welch's Big Trees Resort. This land, which adjoined Cowell's, had belonged to Joseph Welch. In 1930 Welch's family sold it to Santa Cruz County for a county park. When S. H. Cowell decided to give the state his property for a state park, he negotiated successfully with the county and the state to include the Big Trees property in the deal.

29 Laurie MacDougall, *Henry Cowell and His Family (1819—1955)*, p. 28.

Chapter Three – A Santa Cruz Golf Club

1 A number of secondary sources cite Fred Swanton's middle name as Willer; among them: Donald Thomas Clark, *Santa Cruz County Place Names*, p. 550; Charles S. McCaleb, *Surf, Sand & Streetcars*, p. 114; and Richard Hallet, *Never a Dull Moment, Fred Swanton and Santa Cruz, 1882-1940* (San Jose State University thesis, 1976). But his middle name appears as Wilder in the Great Register of Voters, 1886; the IOOF Cemetery Records, September 5, 1940; and General Land Office Certificate No. 19,903, February 19, 1900. These last three citations are definitive.

2 "Another Incorporation," *Sentinel*, April 22, 1890, p. 3.

3 Susan Lehmann, *Fully Developed Context Statement*, p. 7.

4 "The Poles Are Up," *Surf*, June 30, 1906, p. 1; Santa Cruz Seaside Company archives, courtesy of Bonnie Minford, July 11, 2006; "Construction of New Casino," *Surf*, October, 22, 1906, p. 1; "At the Casino," *Surf*, June 15, 1907, p. 1; and "New Casino and Natatorium," *Surf*, June 17, 1907, p. 3.

5 "Cowell Signs Papers For Golf Links Site," *Sentinel*, October 18, 1911, p. 1. This article says the lease was for 125 acres. A subsequent article claims the golf course had 141 acres, *Evening News*, January 18, 1912, p. 1; Susan Lehman in *Fully Developed Context Statement* says 145 acres of land were leased. Perhaps the entire piece of land measured 145 acres with the golf course using 141 acres and the clubhouse area the remaining four acres.

6 "Best Links On Pacific Coast," *Sentinel*, August 18, 1911, p. 1.

7 "M'Cormick Sees Golf Site; Is Enraptured," *Sentinel*, November 7, 1911, p. 1; "Cowell Signs Papers For Golf Links Site," *Sentinel*, October 18, 1911, p. 1; and Rick Hamman, email dated March 3, 2007. Rick is an authority on railroads who wrote the book, *California Central Coast Railways*.

8 "Foundation for E. O. McCormick Residence," *Surf*, April 15, 1912, p. 1; Debra Morstein, *Reflections on Pogonip Perceived, the unveiling of a landscape*, photo captions, Special Collections, University Library, UC Santa Cruz.

9 Historical Notes, Santa Cruz Seaside Company archives; and "At Golf Links," *Surf*, January 13, 1912, p. 1.

10 "Sportiest Golf Club In The West," loose clipping, newpaper and date unknown (Colleen McInerney-Meagher collection).

11 "The New Golf Course," *Surf*, January 18, 1912, p. 1. Bendelow's description of the course corresponds almost exactly to the map printed in the *Sentinel* although some of the yardages differ slightly. It is not clear which is definitive, the map or his description.

12 "Esty Draws Plans For Golf Club House," *Sentinel*, November 11, 1911, p. 4.

13 "Casa Del Rey Links Are Perfect; All Should See Them," *Surf*, February 17, 1912, p. 2.

14 "Esty Draws Plans For Golf Club House."

15 "Golf Club Members To Date," *Surf*, February 17. 1912, p. 3; "Eighty Local Members To New Golf Club," *Evening News*, February 17, 1912, p. 3; and "Golf Tourney Opens Today," *Sentinel*, February 22, 1912, p. 1.

16 Susan Lehmann, *Fully Developed Context Statement*, p. 18.

17 "Golf Tourney Opens Today;" and "Sheep for the Golf Links," *Surf*, May 31, 1912, p. 1.

18 "Fish Pond at Golf Links," *Surf*, April 1, 1912, p. 5. "Casa Del Rey Fish Preserve Feature At Pogonip, *Sentinel*, November 11, 1911, p.9.

19 Walter J. Travis, Ed. *The American Golfer—the Authorative organ of the 'Royal and Ancient Game* (New York: May 1913), pp. 50, 56; and Bonnie Minford, archivist, Santa Cruz Seaside Company, correspondence with authors, July, 11, 2006.

20 "Chamber of Commerce: The Golf Links Up for Discussion," *Surf*, April 5, 1917, p. 4; and "Concerning The Golf Links," *Surf*, April 12, 1917, p. 4.

21 "Santa Cruz Has Splendid Course, But Support Needed," *Evening News*, July 1, 1919, p. 2.

22 "Steps Taken to Improve Golf Links," *Evening News*, February 21,1922, p. 4; and "Installation of Water System…" *Sentinel*, April 12, 1930, p. 8. This article about a new water system says, "the water system was installed in 1925."

23 Roberts, Henry, Ed. *The Green Book of Golf 1923-1924...A Record of Tournaments Held During the Year, Especially in the State of California and an Index of Golfers Located in this Territory.* (San Francisco: Privately Printed, 1923-24), p. 241.

24 Bob Jones had apparently been living at the links. "McCormicks Again Home," *Evening News*, June 22, 1923, p. 2. This article states, "The McCormick home has been occupied by Mr. and Mrs. Bob Jones and family during the absence of the McCormicks."

25 "Nature Aids Santa Cruz Golf Course," *Evening News*, August 22, 1928, p. 1.

26 "Three Plans To Save Golf Club," *Evening News*, December 14, 1929, p. 1; "Cowells Come To Rescue Of The Golf Club," *Sentinel*, December 20, 1929, pp. 1-2; and "Efforts Made To Save Golf Club To City," *Evening News*, December 16, 1929, p. 1.

27 "Fate of Golf Club, "*Evening News*. December 20, 1929, p. 1.

28 "Meet Called In Effort to Revive Old S. C. Golf Club," *Evening News*, April 4, 1933, p. 1.

Notes: Chapter Four – Dorothy Deming Wheeler

1 John Chase, *The Sidewalk Companion to Santa Cruz Architecture, 3rd Edition*, (Santa Cruz: Museum of Art and History, 2005), pp. 16-17.

2 Wally Trabing, "The Grande Dame Of Pogonip," *Sentinel*, September 1, 1972, p. 6.

3 Robin Musitelli, "Return to Glory," *Sentinel*, October 5, 1997, pp. E-1, E-2; photo of Deming House from article by Eleanor Koch, "Santa Cruz Grand Dame To Be Feted Tonight," *Sentinel*, January 22, 1967, p. 12.

4 Deming Stout interview, Lezin Collection, Museum of Art & History, box 471, folder 1.

5 "Deming Wheeler, Head of Pogonip Polo Club, Dies of Heart Attack," *Sentinel*, April 1, 1946, p. 1.

6 Barbara Worth Oakford, *My 70 Year Trip to the Show Jumping Hall of Fame*, (Sacramento: William H. & Barbara W. Oakford, 1997), p. 111.

7 "Wheeler—Deming Wedding," *Surf*, August 28, 1916, p. 4.

8 Conversation with Rachel Torrey, former administrative director at the Santa Cruz Museum of Art and History, an authority on historic dress; November 2004.

9 "Wheeler—Deming Wedding."

10 "Passing of H. S. Deming," obituary for Henry Seth Deming, *Surf*, January 5, 1918, p. 8.

11 "Esteemed Woman of Community Passes Peacefully Away," obituary for Josephine N. Deming, *Evening News*, March 3, 1923, p. 5; and "Services At Family Home," *Sentinel*, March 7, 1923, p. 5.

12 John Chase, *The Sidewalk Companion to Santa Cruz Architecture*, p. 126.

13 "Wheeler Home Burns To Ground," *Evening News*, January 21, 1922, p. 1.

14 "Deming Wheeler, Undaunted By Fire," *Evening News*, May 25, 1922, p. 10.

15 "Roof Weighing 30 Tons," *Evening News*, April 24, 1929, p. 9.

16 Dorothy Deming Wheeler, "Windy Hill Farm," *Country Life*, July 1937, p. 25.

17 Ibid.

18 Conversation with Bob Gillies, May 2005.

Chapter Five – Polo Comes To Santa Cruz

1 "Polo Players Show Class In Weekend Game," *Evening News*, May 14, 1923, p. 2.
2 "New Polo Field To Be Dedicated," *Evening News*, July 7, 1923, p. 2.
3 "Polo Players Show Some Speed," *Evening News*, July 9, 1923, p. 2.
4 "Polo Club Grows As Another Team Goes Into Field," *Evening News*, October 19, 1923, p. 3.
5 "Junior Polo Team Gets Next Chance At Army Players," *Evening News*, October 27, 1923, p. 1.
6 "Tom Mix Likes Polo; Expects To Play Tomorrow," *Evening News*, October 20, 1923, p. 2.
7 "Aptos Field, Beautiful Natural Amphitheater, Dedicated Before Big Crowd," *Evening News*, March 17, 1924, p. 3.
8 "Aptos-Santa Cruz Polo Club Grows With Remarkable Speed," *Evening News*, August 11, 1925, p. 2.
9 "Sunday To Be Gala Day At Aptos Polo Field," *Evening News*, October 16, 1925, p. 2.
10 Hope Swinford, "Membership Grows In The Aptos-Santa Cruz Polo Club, *Evening News*, October 24, 1925, p. 10.
11 Ibid.
12 "Polo Field May Go Is Report," *Evening News*, October 19, 1929, p. 5.
13 David E. Outerbridge, *Champion in a Man's World, the Biography of Marion Hollins* (Chelsea, Michigan: the author, 1998).
14 From the notes of Tanner Wilson, supplied by Bob Beck, former archivist for Pasatiempo.

Chapter Six – The Pogonip Polo Club

1 "New Polo Field And Club Planned," *Evening News*, November 5, 1935, p. 1. The "Henry Cowell" referred to in the article is S. H. Cowell; president of the Henry Cowell Lime and Cement Company.
2 Margaret Koch, "Pogonip—A Look to the Future," *Sentinel*, Nov 4, 1973, p. 16.
3 Dorothy Wheeler, letter to Rose Donnelly, May 13, 1936 (Dorothy Deming Wheeler letters, Colleen McInerney-Meagher collection).
4 Marion Hollins, letter to Rose Donnelly, secretary of the PCWPA, May 3, 1936; and Dorothy Wheeler, letter to Rose Donnelly, May 13, 1936 (Dorothy Deming Wheeler letters).
5 A. N. Goolin, the manager of Pasatiempo, in a letter to Dorothy Wheeler summarizes the amount she had spent on the field in 1935. Periodic bills from Pasatiempo, particularly the bill of July 18, 1935, itemize these expenses. (Dorothy Deming Wheeler letters)
6 Dorothy Deming Wheeler, letter to Gustavo Lombrano, editor of *Sportologue*, January 28, 1936 (Dorothy Deming Wheeler letters).
7 "Pogonip Plans Polo Contests At Santa Cruz," *Evening News*, October 17, 1936, p. 6; and "Pogonip Polo Team Bows To Visiting Four," *Evening News*, October 19, 1936, p. 2.
8 Dorothy Deming Wheeler, letter to Ann Jackson, April 28, 1936 (Dorothy Deming Wheeler letters).
9 Dorothy Deming Wheeler, letter to Ann Jackson, January 6, 1936 (Dorothy Deming Wheeler letters).
10 Mrs. E. Forbes Wilson, article in undated Pogonip brochure (Colleen McInerney-Meagher collection).

Spring Trail hiker.
(James M. Morley)

Chapter Seven – A Very Social Club

1 "New Pool To Open Soon At Pogonip Club," *Evening News*, September 16, 1936, p. 4.
2 Ibid.
3 The Nipper (Bill Irwin), *Pogogoround*, the Pogonip Club newsletter, October 1969.
4 "Pirates Battle On Two Movie Frigates On Bay," *Evening News*, September 16, 1936, p. 4.
5 Rick Chatenever, "Santa Cruz Movie Success No Overnight Sensation," *Sentinel*, July 25, 1980, pp. 15, 24; and "'Salem Maid' Work Starts In Mountains," *Evening News*, September 7, 1936, p. 1.
6 "Stand Up and Fight," http://movies2.nytimes.com/gst/movies/movie.html?v_id=111604.
7 Barbara Worth Oakford, *My 70-Year Trip to the Show Jumping Hall of Fa*me (Sacramento: William H. & Barbara W. Oakford, 1997), p. 193.
8 *Ibid*, p. 195.
9 "M-G-M Unit Completes Work Here," *Evening News*, November 14, 1938, p. 1.
10 "'Salem Maid' Work Starts In Mountains."
11 Mrs. E. Forbes Wilson, article in undated Pogonip brochure.
12 Handwritten notes at end of *Pogogoround* by the Nipper, (Lezin Collection, box 271, folder 1); and Bill Irwin, "Pogonip Polo Club," article for brochure, with handwritten corrections by Elaine McInerney, (Lezin Collection, box 471, folder 1).
13 This quote and the following information about membership are from a letter written by Dorothy Deming Wheeler to Mrs. W. M. Cummings of Watsonville in which she asks Mrs. Cummings to be a committee member to help her select members from 20 Watsonville families (Dorothy Deming Wheeler letters).
14 Classes of Membership (effective January 1, 1952) from the Bylaws of the Pogonip Polo Club, an undated club brochure, but probably 1950 or 1951 (Colleen McInerney-Meagher collection).
15 Doug Baldwin, "Doug-Outs with Doug Baldwin," *Sentinel*, April 21, 1940, p. 7.
16 Mrs. E. Forbes Wilson, article in undated Pogonip brochure.

Chapter Eight – Pogonip At War

1 Dorothy Deming Wheeler, "United States Women's Polo Association," article in unknown magazine, April-May 1942, p. 31, (Dorothy Deming Wheeler scrapbooks).
2 Ibid.
3. "Mounted Troop Gets Start In Santa Cruz," *Sentinel*, June 16, 1942, p. 4.
4 Dorothy Deming Wheeler, "United States Women's Polo Association," p. 19 of unidentified magazine (Colleen McInerney-Meagher collection).
5 "To Form Mounted Corps," unidentified clipping, dated by hand May 1, 1942. (Dorothy Deming Wheeler scrapbooks).
6 Zilfa Estcourt, "Women in War," unidentified news clipping (Dorothy Deming Wheeler scrapbooks).
7 "Horse Parking Lot," headline in newspaper article, dated June 3, 1942. (Dorothy Deming Wheeler scrapbooks).
8 Unidentified clipping (Dorothy Deming Wheeler scrapbooks).
9 *San Francisco Chronicle*, June 14, 1942 (Pat Horton scrapbook).
10 Harley Lewis, Red Cross correspondent, *Riptide*, Santa Cruz, August 11, 1944, p. 1,
11 "Horseback Therapy," *Click* magazine, August 1944, pp. 55-57.
12 "Crashed Plane At Pogonip…," *Sentinel*, April 8, 1944, p. 1; and "Red Cross First Aider on Scene Of Plane Crash," unidentified clipping (Dorothy Wheeler scrapbooks).

Chapter Nine - Pogonip Carries On

1 Unidentified clippings report on a series of games in the spring and summer of 1947 (Colleen McInerney-Meagher collection).
2 "Pogonip Polo Players Win From Visitors," *Sentinel-News*, July 6, 1947, p. 13.
3 See Chapter 8, "Pogonip At War," for a description of this incident.
4 Unidentified clipping , May 7, 1948 (Colleen McInerney-Meagher collection).

5 "150 At Dinner-Dance Marking Re-opening of Pogonip Club," *Sentinel*, June 1, 1948, p. 2.

6 List of Pogonip Presidents (1948 to 1986) (Lezin Collection, box 471, folder 1); "Pogonip Polo Club Elects Tanner Wilson," *Sentinel*, September 30, 1951.

7 "Deming Wheeler, Head Of Pogonip Polo Club, Dies Of Heart Attack," *Sentinel*, April 1, 1946, p. 1.

8 Dorothy Deming Wheeler scrapbooks; and "Mrs. D. Wheeler Back From S. A.," *Sentinel*, May 3, 1948.

9 "Mrs. Wheeler Was Married Saturday Eve," *Sentinel*, Sept. 28, 1949, p. 3.

10 Bill Irwin obituary in the *Nipper*, the Pogonip Club newsletter, undated but shortly after Dorothy's death (Colleen McInerney-Meagher collection).

11 Eleanor Koch, "Santa Cruz' Grande Dame To Be Feted," *Sentinel*, January 22, 1967, p. 12; and "Pogonip Founder To Be Honored," *Sentinel*, January 21, 1971, p. 4; "Dorothy and Her Party," *Sentinel*, January 22, 1974, p. 6.

12 Bill Irwin obituary in the *Nipper*.

13 "Dorothy Wilson, 80, Pogonip Founder, Dies," *Sentinel*, March 23, 1975, p. 1.

14 "150 At Dinner-Dance Marking Re-opening of Pogonip Club;" "Pogonip Polo Club Elects Tanner Wilson;" "Pogonip Names New Directors, Plans Events," *Sentinel*, September 12, 1952, p. 3; "New Officers Are Named For Pogonip, *Sentinel*, August 29, 1955, p. 3.

15 Logo appears on folder announcing the agenda for the September 26, 1986 board meeting (Lezin collection, box 473, folder 10) and on the 1990 Brochure for new clubhouse (Colleen McInerney-Meagher collection) among many other examples.

16 Letter to the Cowell trustees from Pogonip (Lezin Collection, box 471, folder 1). This letter refers to a forthcoming Sunday article in the *Sentinel* devoted to Pogonip; the *Sentinel* devoted two Sunday sections to articles on Pogonip by Margaret Koch: "Pogonip – A Look to the Future," *Sentinel*, November 4, 1973 and "Pogonip – polo or fog?" *Sentinel*, November 18, 1973. By inference, the letter was written in early November 1973.

17 "Tree 'n Sea Living," *Sentinel*, February 13, 1974, p. 8.

18 Conversation with Marta Gaines, August 2006.

19 Statement in "Pogonip By Laws," 1984 (Lezin Collection, box 472, folder 8).

20 Sam Ober, letter to members, April 1986 (Lezin collection, box 472, folder 8).

21 Contract between Pogonip Polo Club and Warner Bros. (Lezin collection, box 472, folder 5).

22 "The Lost Boys (1987)," http://www.fast-rewind.com, viewed February 2006.

23 "A city's reputation at stake," *San Jose Mercury-News*, undated clipping (Colleen McInerney-Meagher collection).

24 "Teen-age Vampires Pose No Threat to SC Image," *Good Times*, August 6, 1987, pp. 5-6.

25 "The Lost Boys (1987)," http://www.fast-rewind.com, viewed February 2006.

26 A copy of this historic newsreel is available at Special Collections, University Library, UCSC.

27 When the Pogonip clubhouse closed in 1987, the exhibit, still mounted for its fiftieth anniversary, was moved to the Octagon Museum. The exhibit, greatly enhanced and titled "Comin' Thu," opened in January 1988 and continued into February 1988.

28 Christina Waters, "POGONIP: The Future Is Wide Open," *Pacific Magazine*, May 1989, p. 18.

29 "County condemns Pogonip clubhouse" by Joan Raymond, *Sentinel*, February 10, 1987, p. A-4.

30 Christina Waters, "POGONIP: The Future Is Wide Open," p. 14.

31 Club attorney David Baskin quoted in article by Martha Mendoza, "Pogonip Polo Club is calling it quits," *Sentinel*, October 14, 1993, p. A-6.

32 Margaret Koch, "Pogonip—A Look To The Future," *Sentinel*, November 4, 1973, p. 16.

Chapter Ten – Sycamore Grove Camp

1 Sharon Christensen, "Sycamore Grove," a personal memoir by a granddaughter of Philip and Ethel Fridley, managers of Sycamore Grove Camp; and a phone conversation with Sharon Christensen on March 4, 2007.

2 Donald Thomas Clark, *Santa Cruz County Place Names*, p. 363.

3 Sharon Christensen, phone conversation, February 9, 2007; and "Answers to some

questions about my grandparents and the grove," March 22, 2007.

4 "Mrs. Fridley, Loved Woman Passes Away," obituary for Salome Fridley, *Evening News*, August 29, 1927, p. 8; and Leon Rowland Card Files Box A-4 Card 394.

5 Leon Rowland Card Files box A-4 card 1054; box A-6 card 514; box A-6 card 261; box A-6 card 51; and box A-1 card 562.01.

6 *Sentinel* December 22, 1877, p. 2; *Sentinel*, May 22, 1866, p. 2; and Leon Rowland Card Files, box A-4 card 537.01.

7 "Mrs. Fridley, Loved Woman Passes Away;" and Phyllis Fridley Tuma, "Our Family History, A Swimming Hole – A Dream," hand-written memoir (Sharon Christensen collection).

8 Phyllis Fridley Tuma, "Our Family History."

9 Leon Rowland Card Files, box A-6 card 200.02; and Sharon Christensen phone conversation February 10, 2007.

10 "Fridley-Redding," *Surf*, April 24, 1906, p.1; and Phyllis Fridley Tuma, "Our Family History."

11 Susan Lehmann, *Fully Developed Context Statement*, p. 19.

12 Sharon Christensen, "Answers to some questions." The exact birth dates of Robert and Dan are not known to the family, but they were listed in the 1930 census as ages twelve and eleven, respectively.

13 Vernon Fridley, Jr., "Memories of Sycamore Grove," hand-written memoir, February 8, 2007. Vernon is a grandson of Philip and Ethel Fridley; Sharon Christensen, phone conversation March 4, 2007.

14 Ibid.

15 Ibid.

16 Sharon Christensen, phone conversations February and March 2007.

17 Sharon Christensen, "Sycamore Grove;" and Barry Brown, historian of Paradise Park, email November 13, 2006.

18 Sharon Christensen, "Sycamore Grove."

19 Vernon Fridley, Jr., "Memories of Sycamore Grove."

20 Phyllis Fridley Tuma, "Our Family History;" Vernon Fridley, Jr. "Memories of Sycamore Grove;" and "At Key West," *Sentinel*, May 5, 1954, p. 5.

21 Vernon Fridley, Jr. "Memories of Sycamore Grove;" and "Fridley," *Sentinel*, May 24, 1944, p. 4.

22 "Parents Get Medals For Bob Fridley," *Sentinel*, April 20, 1945, p. 1; and "Three S.C. Hero Dead Returning To Burial Here," *Sentinel*, February 6, 1949, p. 2.

23 Phyllis Fridley Tuma, "Our Family History."

24 Carolyn Swift, "The Flood Terror of 1955," *Sentinel*, November 4, 2001, p. A-12.

25 "Heart Attack Is Fatal To Philip Fridley," *Sentinel*, December 24, 1955, p. 12; and Sharon Christensen, phone conversation March 4, 2007.

26 Wally Trabing, "Valley Suffers Severe Damage As Flood Rages," *Sentinel*, December 25, 1955, p. 1.

27 Cowell Ranch Records, July 1950 through March 1956 (S. H. Cowell Foundation Ledgers, MS 80 Box 16, Special Collections, University Library, UC Santa Cruz).

28 Noel Patterson letter to Mr. Connick of the Cowell Foundation, April 17, 1961 (Hihn-Younger Archives, Box 39, NP A22-E, Special Collections, University Library, UC Santa Cruz).

29 Susan Lehmann, *Fully Developed Context Statement*, p. 19.

30 "Ethel Fridley Dies At Age 80," *Sentinel*, April 15, 1968, p. 14. We have not discovered exactly when the camp closed, but it was probably in 1965.

Chapter Eleven – Pogonip and the City

1 Bill Neubauer, "Will SC Get Into Realty Business?," *Sentinel*, December 1, 1977, p. 1; and Bill Neubauer, "Diverse, Loaded General Plan Suggestions Go To SC Council," *Sentinel*, April 7, 1978, p. 21.

2 Sydney Williams, A.I.P, *Sketch General Plan Santa Cruz, California, Santa Cruz of Tomorrow Citizens Committee, Summary of Final Report*, Government Publications, University Library, UC Santa Cruz, 1960, p. 2.

3 "Pogonip Foes Flex, Prepare To Fight," *Sentinel*, March 31, 1978, p. 21.

4 Bill Neubauer, "Planner Says Pogonip Annexation Necessary," *Sentinel*, April 7, 1978, p. 1; and Bill Neubauer, "Diverse, Loaded General Plan Suggestions Go To SC Council."

5 Wally Trabing, "One Candle For Pogonip," *Sentinel*, May 4, 1978, p. 13.

6 Bill Neubauer, "Will Pogonip Annexation Meet Local Housing Needs?," *Sentinel*, June 7, 1978, p. 36.

7 Ibid.

8 "The 1970s," *Sentinel* Online Edition (http://www.santacruzsentinel.com/extra/century/71).

9 "SC Council Refuses To Place 'Greenbelt' Issue on Ballot," Sentinel, March 14, 1979, pp. A1, A6.

10 "The 1970s," Sentinel Online Edition.

11 "Pogonip Owners Threaten Suit," *Sentinel*, March 7, 1980, p. 2.

12 Joan Raymond, "Pogonip: Where does it go from here?," *Sentinel*, June 10, 1984, pp. A1, A6; and Stephanie Hauk interviewed by Sam Mitchell in "Legacy of Unspoilt Land," *The News*, February 21, 1985, p. 1.

13 Joan Raymond, "POGONIP/Plans for pristine parcel…," *Sentinel*, May 16, 1986, p. A-5.

14 Joan Raymond, "Pogonip proposal could go to voters," *Sentinel*, February 4, 1987, p. A1.

15 Ibid.

16 Quote taken from "Pogonip—Serenity and Controversy" by Nona P. Pierce, *Coastal HOMES Magazine*, November 7, 1984, p. 9.

17 Jennifer Koss, "Future of Pogonip property…,"*Sentinel*, October 26, 1984, p. A-6.

18 Joan Raymond, "Pogonip—Where does it go from here?" and Sam Mitchell, "Legacy of Unspoilt Land."

19 Joan Raymond, "Housing and parkland may be in Pogonip's future," *Sentinel*, March 22, 1987, p. A-4.

20 Conversation with Andrew Schiffrin, October 2, 2006.

21 Joan Raymond, "Initiative embraces Pogonip purchase," *Sentinel*, April 27, 1987, pp. A-1, A-12; Paul Beatty, "Chamber backs park in Pogonip," *Sentinel*, May 8, 1987, p. A-4; and Jennifer Koss, "Agreement near on Pogonip's future," *Register-Pajaronian*, September 5, 1987, p. 1.

22 Katharine Ball, "Pogonip preservation initiative on ballot," *Register-Pajaronian*, November 12, 1987, p. 1; and Tom Long, "State vote may mean Pogonip park" *Sentinel*, November 13, 1987, p. 1.

23 Paul Beatty, "Chamber backs park in Pogonip."

24 Guy Lasnier, "Escrow closes on SC's Pogonip deal, *Register-Pajaronian*, April 5, 1989; and Donald Miller, "Pogonip Purchase Hurdle Cleared," *Sentinel*, April 6, 1989, p. A-5.

25 Christina Waters, "POGONIP: The Future Is Wide Open," p. 17.

Chapter Twelve – The Clubhouse Controversy

1 A Xerox copy of this report is part of the Harriet Deck collection of Historical Trust documents.

2 Christina Waters, "POGONIP: The Future Is Wide Open," p. 18.

3 Colleen McInerney-Meagher, letter to Ms. Sara Kane of the Historic Preservation Commission, July 17, 1989 (Historical Trust documents, Harriet Deck collection).

4 State of California, Department of Parks and Recreation, Historic Resources Inventory, undated but later than 1988 from internal evidence (Historical Trust documents).

5 Colleen McInerney-Meagher, letters to the Santa Cruz City Council, October 10, 1989 and to the Historic Preservation Commission, November 3, 1989 and January 16, 1990 (Historical Trust documents).

6 Mark Bergstrom, "Pogonip club revival under way, "*Sentinel*, March 8, 1990, p. A-2.

7 Mark Bergstrom, "New Pogonip Club will look familiar," *Sentinel*, August 3, 1990, p. A-2.

8 Brochure issued by the "new" Pogonip Polo Club to attract new members, undated, probably 1990 (Colleen McInerney collection).

9 Colleen McInerney-Meagher, letter to the editor, *Sentinel*, April 22, 1990 (Colleen

McInerney-Meagher collection).

10 Public Notice, *Sentinel*, September 2,1990 (Harriet Deck Historical Trust documents).

11 Douglas Deitch, letter to SC City Council, September 10, 1990; and Colleen McInerney-Meagher, letter to Santa Cruz Historical Trust, September 13, 1990 (Harriet Deck Historical Trust documents).

12 "Council extends Pogonip Lease," *Sentinel*, January 10, 1991, p. A-2.

13 Mark Bergstrom, "Pogonip Club wants new house," *Sentinel*, March 18, 1991, p. A-2.

14 Ibid.

15 Marti Christoffer of Christoffer Associates, letter to Sara Ray of the Historic Preservation Commission, March 18, 1991 (Colleen McInerney-Meagher collection).

16 Steve Perez, "Pogonip clubhouse demolition OK'd," *Sentinel*, March 21, 1991, p. A-5; and Karen Clark, "Pogonip Clubhouse hearing delayed," *Sentinel*, May 15, 1991. p. A-6.

17 "Proposed clubhouse dealt setback," *Sentinel*, March 30, 1991, p. A-2.

18 Karen Clark, "Pogonip Clubhouse hearing delayed."

19 John Bessa, "Designs on Pogonip," *Sentinel*, August 9, 1992, p. A-2.

20 Ibid.

21 Ibid.

22 Martha Mendoza, "Old clubhouse ready for facelift," *Sentinel*, December 6, 1992, p. A-10.

23 Martha Mendoza, "Pogonip Polo Club is calling it quits," *Sentinel*, October 14, 1993, pp. A-1, A-6.

24 Jeremy Lezin, letter to Richard Wilson, City Manager, October 17, 1993, (Historical Trust documents).

Chapter Thirteen – The City Makes Plans

1 "City Council fills out Pogonip Task Force," *Sentinel*, September 25, 1991, p. A-2; and Karen Clark, "Public hearing set on Pogonip," *Sentinel*, December 13, 1991, p. A-7.

2 Teresa Jimenez, "Pogonip committee faces balancing act," *Sentinel*, December 15, 1991, p. A-4.

3 Robert Pollie, "Pogonip too beautiful to risk destroying with broad developments," *Sentinel*, November 22, 1992, p. A-17.

4 Martha Mendoza, "Pogonip Decision Day," *Sentinel*, January 25, 1993, p. A-2; and Martha Mendoza, "Footing the Bill," *Sentinel*, December 6, 1992, p. A-10.

5 Harry Mok, "Museum officials make a pitch for Pogonip site," *Sentinel*, June 6, 1991, p. A-3.

6 Robert Stephens, "Natural history museum would complement Pogonip," *Sentinel*, November 22, 1992, p. A-17.

7 Martha Mendoza, "Pogonip: decision day," p. A-2

8 Harry Mok, "Museum officials make a pitch for Pogonip site."

9 Cynthia Mills, "Grass-roots solution," *Sentinel*, December 6, 1992, p. A-10.

10 Joseph E. Patten, "Pogonip area lost its 'natural state' long ago," letter to the editor, *Sentinel*, November 22, 1992, p. A-17.

11 Martha Mendoza, "Pogonip: decision day," *Sentinel*, January 25, 1993, p. A-2.

12 Martha Mendoza, "Footing the Bill," p. A-10.

13 Martha Mendoza, "Some say land should be used for recreation," *Sentinel*, December 6, 1992, p. A-12.

14 Martha Mendoza, "Pogonip choices pared," *Sentinel*, January 27, 1993, p. A-1.

15 Robin Musitelli, "SC rejects proposal for new Pogonip Club," *Sentinel*, May 12, 1995, A-1.

16 Ibid.

17 Minutes of the Santa Cruz City Council meeting of January 28, 1997. The purchase price was $600,000 and was paid to Wave Crest Development, Inc. and Lawrence and Douglas Michels.

18 "Pogonip Final Master Plan," City of Santa Cruz Parks and Recreation Department, July 1998, pp. 2-3, 2-4.

19 John Woolfolk, "Historic clubhouse gets a lift," *San Jose Mercury News*, April 14, 2000, p. 1.

20 California Register of Historical Resources, June 4, 2001.

21 Dan White, "Another go at Pogonip," *Sentinel*, April 20, 2001, p. A-1.

22 Dan White, "State gives $500K to Pogonip," Sentinel, April 28, 2001.

23 Karen Clark, "Non-hikers may have to cool heels on Pogonip," *Sentinel*, June 21, 1997, p. A-2.

24 Karen Clark, "Council waits on opening up trails," *Sentinel*, June 25, 1997.

25 Francine Taylor, *Currents*, University of California, Santa Cruz web site. viewed January 2006.

26 Lara Wallentine, "Trail spans Pogonip," *Sentinel*, June 20, 1999, p. A-4.

27 Ibid

28 Karen Clark, "Visions clash. Community debates Pogonip land use," *Sentinel*, April 1, 1998, p. A-1.

29 Robin Musitelli, "Commission's Pogonip plan restricts use," *Sentinel*, July 9, 1998, p. A-1; and "Pogonip plan keeps bikes, horses at bay," *Sentinel*, July 10, 1998, p. A-2.

30 Lynne Baseshore Cooper, "Pogonip Update," address to City Council, July 20, 1998, Homeless Garden Project History, web site: http://www.homelessgardenproject.org/history.html.

31 Ibid.

32 Heather Boerner, "A Road Less Traveled," *Sentinel*, October 19, 2003, p. A-1.

33 Ibid, p. A-10.

34 Ibid, p. A-10.

35 Brian Seals, "City: No access road through Pogonip," *Sentinel*, December 11, 2003, p. A-4.

36 "Pogonip's grassy hills a magnet to trespassers," *Register-Pajaronian*, September, 5, 1987, p. 13.

Chapter Fourteen - Pogonip Today

1 City of Santa Cruz Parks and Recreation Department brochure, available at sign shelters by the two main entrances, is the source for the trail map and for information about Pogonip habitats and wildlife. This information can also be found on the web site: http://www.santacruzparksandrec.com/parks/pogo.html.

2 Frank A. Perry, et al., pp. 8-12

3 David W. Andersen and Michael J. Rymer, eds., *Tectonics and Sedimentation Along Faults of the San Andreas System*, (Los Angeles: The Pacific Section, Society of Economic Paleontologists and Mineralogists, 1983), pp. 80-81; and Frank Perry, et. al., *Lime Kiln Legacies*, p. 210.

4 David W. Andersen and Michael J. Rymer, eds., *Tectonics and Sedimentation Along Faults of the San Andreas System*, pp. 79-80.

5 Frank A. Perry, "Probing Pogonip's Past," notes for a class on Pogonip's geology, 1991.

6 David Suddjian, "Santa Cruz Birds," *The Albatross*, Vol. 49A, No. 1, September – October 2004; reporting on sightings between March 15 and May 31, 2004.

Chapter Fifteen – Exploring Pogonip

1 *Pogonip Final Master Plan* (Santa Cruz: City of Santa Cruz Parks and Recreation Department, 1998) provides much of the information for this chapter on trails and wildlife. The maps in this chapter are derived from the map found at each park entrance kiosk.

2 Sheridan F. Warrick, ed., *The Natural History of the UC Santa Cruz Campus* (Santa Cruz: Environmental Field Program, University of California at Santa Cruz, 1982), p. 127; reference to B. L. Gordon, *Monterey Bay Area: Natural History and Cultural Imprints*. (Pacific Grove: Boxwood Press, 1977)

3 Sheridan F. Warrick, ed., *The Natural History of the UC Santa Cruz Campus*, p. 24.

4 Paul Lee, http://www.ecotopia.org/trail/oak.html, viewed November 2005. Paul Lee is an Episcopal minister who lives in Santa Cruz and who was active in preserving Pogonip as a greenbelt. He is also an advocate for the homeless and is author of, *The Quality Of Mercy, Homelessness in Santa Cruz*, (Santa Cruz: Platonic Academy Press, 1985).

5 Patricia Doler recalls that what is now called Redwood Creek was once called Rincon Creek.

6 Frank A. Perry, et al., *Lime Kiln Legacies*, p. 76.

7 Celia Scott provided the one vote to preserve the redwoods. In an earlier debate, she remarked: "The lesson of history is that the kilns destroyed the redwoods, and now the

redwoods are coming back. You could call it poetic justice;" "Kill the Kilns," *Sentinel*, July 2, 1996, pp. A-1, A-10; and Karen Clark, "SC council approves removal of redwoods..." *Sentinel*, July 10, 1996, pp. A-1, A-8.

8   Francine Taylor, *Currents*, University of California, Santa Cruz web site; and conversation with Vivian Beebe, Chuck Beebe's widow, March 31, 2007.

9   Mark Lawshe, "Ghost Story of Sarah Cowell," *Sentinel*, October 30, 1975, p. 23; and "Fatal Accident," *Morning Sentinel*, May 15, 1903, p. 3.

10 1912 maps and 1923 map of golf links show the name Pogonip Avenue (Map Room, University Library, UC Santa Cruz). Maps when the club was called Pogonip show the name Golf Club Drive. A 1971 City Map issued by the County Bank of Santa Cruz and maps provided by the City of Santa Cruz Parks and Recreation Department show the name Golf Club Drive.

11 "Shawn Brayshaw," obituary, Sentinel, December 9, 1990, p. A-17.

12 *A Legal History of Santa Cruz County* (Santa Cruz: Museum of Art & History, 2006), pp. 96,97.

13 Debra Morstein, *Remembrance of Pogonip's Past-An Historical Overv*iew (San Francisco: S.H. Cowell Foundation, 1987). Caption to photograph of elk.

14 Conversation with Norman Gotti, March 11, 2007.

15 After the McCormick family ceased to use the house, it apparently reverted to the Cowells. Cowell Ranch records from the 1950s show that the ranch received $50 per month rent for the McCormick house from Kate Remington. (Cowell Ranch Records, July 1950 through March 1956, MS 80 Box 16, Special Collections, University Library, UC Santa Cruz); and "Foundation For E. O. McCormick Residence," *Surf*, April 15,1912, p. 1.

16 R. L. Polk & Co. directories for the years 1948 through 1960; and conversation with Patricia Doler, whose father, Ken Doler, knew Kate Remington, October 15, 2006.

17 Before the stables were demolished, the Santa Cruz County Historical Trust commissioned a set of architectural plans, watercolor drawings, and photographs of the stables. These are in the Museum of Art & History archives.

18 "Natural Resources," *Pogonip Final Master Plan*, 5-5.

19 Ibid.

Metal basins across Spring Trail from cement water trough,.possibly used to water teams of oxen. (Joan Gilbert Martin)

Resources

Books

Bancroft, Hubert Howe. *History of California*. San Francisco: A. L. Bancroft, 1884-90.
— *Register of Pioneer Inhabitants of California, 1542-1848, and index to information concerning them in Bancroft's History of California, volumes I –V*. Los Angeles: Dawson's Book Shop, 1964.

Clark, Donald Thomas. *Santa Cruz County Place Names, A Geographical Dictionary*. Santa Cruz: Santa Cruz Historical Society, 1986.

Hamman, Rick. *California Central Coast Railways*. Santa Cruz: Otter B Books, 2002.

History of Alameda County, California. Oakland: M.W. Wood, 1883

Hodge, Frederick Webb, ed. *Handbook of American Indians, North of Mexico*. Washington, D. C.: Bureau of American Ethnology, 1907.

Kroeber, Alfred L. *Handbook of Indians of California*. New York: Dover Publications, 1976.

Lehman, Susan. *Fully Developed Context Statement for the City of Santa Cruz*. Santa Cruz: City of Santa Cruz Planning and Community Development Department, 2000.

MacDougall, Laurie. *Henry Cowell and His Family (1819-1955): A Brief History*. San Francisco: S. H. Cowell Foundation, 1989.

Margolin, Malcolm. *The Ohlone Way, Indian life in the San Francisco-Monterey Bay Area*. Berkeley: California, Heyday Books, 1978.

Martin, Edward. *History of Santa Cruz County, California with Biographical Sketches*. Los Angeles: Historic Record Company, 1911.

McCaleb, Charles S. *Surf, Sand & Streetcars, A Mobile History of Santa Cruz, California*, 2nd printing. Santa Cruz: Museum of Art & History, 2005.

Oakford, Barbara Worth. *My 70 Year Trip to the Show Jumping Hall of Fame*. Sacramento: William H. & Barbara W. Oakford, 1997.

Outerbridge, David E. *Champion in a Man's World, the Biography of Marion Hollins*. Chelsea, Michigan: David E. Outerbridge, 1998.

Perry, Frank, Robert A. Piwarzyk, Michael D. Luther, Alverda Orlando, Allan Molho, and Sierra L. Perry. *Lime Kiln Legacies, The History of the Lime Industry in Santa Cruz County*. Santa Cruz: Museum of Art & History, 2007.

Roberts, Henry, ed. *The Green Book of Golf...A Record of Tournaments Held During the Year, Especially in the State of California and an Index of Golfers Located in this Territory*. San Francisco: Ellis & Roberts, 1923-24.

Rowland, Leon. *Santa Cruz, The Early Years*. Santa Cruz: Paper Vision Press, 1980.

Warrick, Sheridan, ed. *The Natural History of the UC Santa Cruz Campus*. Santa Cruz: Environmental Field Program, UC Santa Cruz, 1982.

Yamane, Linda, ed. *A Gathering of Voices, The Native Peoples of the Central California Coast, Santa Cruz County History Journal, No. 5*. Santa Cruz: Museum of Art & History, 2002.

Journals and Magazines

"California's Pioneer Wine Families." *California Historical Society Quarterly*, vol. 54.

Dunaway, Douglas. "Seeing through the fog – Unraveling the mystery of poconip [sic]." *Mono Lake Newsletter*, Spring 2006, pp. 16, 18.

Foote, Robert Ordway. "Women's Polo in the West." *The Horse*. January-February, 1936.

"Horseback Therapy." *Click* magazine, August 1944. pp. 55-57.

Lewis, Harley. Photo essay on the Women's Mounted Unit of the Santa Cruz Red Cross. *Riptide*, Vol. 13, No. 6, August 11, 1944. pp. 1, 3, 4.

McCracken, Josephine. "The Home Ranch of the Cowells." *Overland Monthly*, July 1912. pp. 17-23.

Pierce, Nona P. "Pogonip—Serenity and Controversy." *Coastal HOMES Magazine*, November 7, 1984.

Suddjian, David. "Santa Cruz Birds." *The Albatross*, Vol. 49A, No. 1, September – Oct. 2004.

Travis, Walter J., ed. *The American Golfer—the Authorative organ of the 'Royal and Ancient Game*, May 1913. pp. 50, 56.

Waters, Christina. "Pogonip, A Sense of Place." *Taste* magazine, June 24, 1986.

— "POGONIP: The Future Is Wide Open." *Pacific Magazine*, May 1989. pp.14-18.

Weston, Sarah. "The Aptos Polo Grounds – Where Sport Was King at Least for a Brief Moment." *The Aptos Almanac*, 2005/2006.

Maps

Baldwin, Arnold M. *City of Santa Cruz*. 1923. No.12 shows Santa Cruz Golf & Country Club including pond & path from Links Station to Club House. Nos.14 & 15 show relation of Fridley ranch to Cowell Ranch house. Call number: G 4364.S69 G46 1925 B25. (Map Room, University Library, UC Santa Cruz)

[*Casa del Rey Golf Links*]. 1912? Map of 18 holes of the golf course. Shows trail from Links station to First Tee & Clubhouse. Call number: G 4364.S69:2 P6 1912? A8. (Map Room, University Library, UC Santa Cruz)

Lewis, William J. *Rancho de la Canada del Rincon en el Ro San Lorenzo de Sta. Cruz, Finally confirmed to Don Pedro Sansevaine* [sic]. 1855. Call numbers: G 4363.S5:2 R32 G46 1855.L4. (Special Collections, University Library, UC Santa Cruz)

Milliken, Randall. *General locations of triblet territories in the Monterey Bay Area*. (Western Anthropological Research Group, Inc., Davis, California)

[*Ohlone Language Groups*]. *Gathering of Voices, The Native Peoples of the Central California Coast*. 2002. (Museum of Art & History, Santa Cruz)

[*Plat of Cowell Foundation lands, Santa Cruz County*]. 1961. Shows campus site & Henry Cowell State Park. Call number: G 4364.S69:2 U6 1961 P6. (Map Room, University Library, UC Santa Cruz)

Pogonip Park. 1993. Shows roads, kilns, trails, railroad, gates. Call number: G4364.S69.2 PL 1993 536. (Map Room, University Library, UC Santa Cruz)

Pogonip. 1999. Official park map from Pogonip Brochure. (City of Santa Cruz Parks and Recreation Department)

United States Geological Survey. *Santa Cruz Quadrangle*. Edition of 1902 (surveyed in 1895 and 1899). Shows ranchos called Refugio, Cañada del Rincón, La Carbonera, Zayante, and San Augustin. Call number: G3700 svar .U6 Case D. (Earth Sciences & Map Library, UC Berkeley)

Miscellaneous Publications

Morstein, Debra. *Remembrance of Pogonip's Past, An Historical Overview.* Photographic essay. San Francisco: S. H. Cowell Foundation, December 1987. (Special Collections, University Library, UC Santa Cruz)

— *Reflections on Pogonip Perceived, the unveiling of a landscape.* Photo captions. 1987. (Special Collections, University Library, UC Santa Cruz)

Santa Cruz City Directories. San Francisco: R. L. Polk & Co. 1927 through 1971. (University Library, UC Santa Cruz)

Supreme Court of United States. *The California Powder Works; Plaintiff in Error vs. Willis Davis, Administrator of the Estate of Isaac E. Davis, Deceased and Henry Cowell.* Record Case No 14,346, October Term, 1893, Term No. 301. (Special Collections, University Library, UC Santa Cruz)

Williams, Sydney, A.I.P, *Sketch General Plan Santa Cruz, California, Santa Cruz of Tomorrow Citizens Committee, Summary of Final Report*, Government Publications. 1960. (University Library, UC Santa Cruz)

Unpublished Documents, Reports, and Oral Histories

Calciano, Elizabeth Spelling. *Random Notes on the Cowell Family and Ranch*, 1971. (Santa Cruz Public Library Clipping File)

Cardiff, George H. *Santa Cruz and the Cowell Ranch, 1890-1964.* Interview by Elizabeth Spedding Calciano. 1965. (University Library, UC Santa Cruz)

Cowell, S. H. Cowell Ledgers, July 1950 through March 1956. Cowell Ranch Records, MS 80 Box 16. (Special Collections, University Library, UC Santa Cruz)

Dorothy Deming Wheeler letters (Colleen McInerney-Meagher collection)

Fehliman, Clinton. E. "Economic history of Santa Cruz County, California, 1850-1947." (Special Collections, University Library, UC Santa Cruz).

Fridley, Vernon, Jr. "Memories of Sycamore Grove," February 8, 2007. (Sharon Christensen collection)

Hallet, Richard. *Never a Dull Moment, Fred Swanton and Santa Cruz, 1882-1940.* Thesis. 1976. (San Jose State University)

Jensen, Kenneth. *The lime industry in Santa Cruz County.* Master's thesis, San Jose State University. 1976. (Special Collections, University Library, UC Santa Cruz)

Rowland, Leon, card files. (Special Collections, University Library, UC Santa Cruz)

Tuma, Phyllis Fridley," Our Family History, A Swimming Hole – A Dream." (Sharon Christensen collection)

Scrapbooks

Horton, Pat. (Colleen McInerney-Meagher collection)

McHugh, Thomas. (Special Collections, University Library, UC Santa Cruz)

McInerney, Elaine. (Colleen McInerney-Meagher collection)

Ober, Verna B. and Sam. (Lezin Collection, Museum of Art & History @ McPherson Center)

Rand, Barbara. (Colleen McInerney-Meagher collection)

Wheeler, Dorothy Deming. (Special Collections, University Library, UC Santa Cruz)

Index

U-Con Trail.
(Joan Gilbert Martin)

Acknowledgements

We would like to thank the following people for their help with this book. And we would like to add that any errors are ours, not theirs.

We thank the current staff at Special Collections of the University Library at UC Santa Cruz: Christine Bunting, Gretchen Dempewolf, and Luisa Orlando, as well as Rita Bottoms, Carole Champion, and Paul Stubbs, now retired, all of whom were unfailingly gracious in finding documents, photographs, and ephemera; Amy Dunning of the Museum of Art & History, who gave us access to the Lezin collection and who found invaluable photographs in the Museum of Art & History archives; and we thank the City of Santa Cruz Parks and Recreation Department for all their support.

We thank our fellow researchers, including the members of Researcher's Anonymous at the Museum of Art & History. In particular, we thank: Stanley D. Stevens, who was always ready to help us locate source material, who found maps when no one else could, and who bravely read the entire first draft; Douglas J. Petersen, who read the chapter on "Native Peoples" and made important suggestions; and Allen Lönnberg who helped with his knowledge of Ohlone tribal sites; Randall Milliken, who allowed us to use his map; Frank A. Perry, who gave unstintingly of his time, shared his extensive knowledge of the Cowell family and their lime interests, and who read the final draft; Bonnie Minford and Brigid Fuller of the Seaside Company, who provided information from their archives and who read "A Santa Cruz Golf Club;" Bob Beck, archivist for Pasatiempo; and Neil Hotelling, Pebble Beach historian who helped with the chapter on golf.

We also thank: Bob Gillies, Bill Whitney, Carole Ehrhardt (granddaughter of Grace Douglas), and William H. Oakford (husband of the late Barbara Worth) for their memories of women's polo at the Pogonip Polo Club; Harriet Deck, Marta Gaines, and Ann Marie Suchman, for their memories of the Pogonip Country Cub in the 1970s and 1980s, and Sally Franks for reading "Pogonip carries On" as well as the chapters on Pogonip and the City of Santa Cruz; Sharon Christensen, who generously provided photographs and documents of the Fridley family and the camp at Sycamore Grove, and who, with her brother Philip Tuma, drew the map of the grove; Vernon Fridley, Jr., whose memories of summers at the grove brought those days to life; John Lisher, Andy Schiffrin, and Celia Scott, who fleshed out the story of the struggle by the city of Santa Cruz to buy the Pogonip property and then decide what to do with it; Harriet Deck for letting us use her Santa Cruz County Historical Trust documents regarding the Pogonip clubhouse; and Robley Levy, for reading the chapters on "Pogonip and the City."

Patricia Doler deserves thanks for her help with "Exploring Pogonip;" her guidance through the trails and meadows of Pogonip made this last chapter possible. We also thank Kevin Whitlock, a forestry consultant, who helped with tree identification.

Many people contributed photographs: James M. Morley, who took photographs of Pogonip as we walked the trails; Don Nielsen, whose photographs originally appeared in the Department of Parks and Recreation brochure for Pogonip; Dan Coyro, Don Fukuda, Bill Lovejoy, and Schmuel Thaler, whose photographs over the years graced the *Sentinel* and other local publications; Dennis Redmond for his photographs of life at Sycamore Grove Camp; Debra Morstein Sloss, for the use of her photograph from "Remembrance of Pogonip's Past;" and Rick Hyman, Ronnie Trubeck, and Geoffrey Dunn who allowed us to reproduce photographs and postcards from their collections.

About the Authors

Joan Gilbert Martin has been a technical writer and a high school history teacher. After moving to Santa Cruz in 1966, she became interested in local history, an interest that spanned three generations: her mother, Grace Gilbert, was a volunteer for the Santa Cruz County Historical Trust and her daughter, Rachel McKay, was for many years archivist and research librarian with the Museum of Art & History at the McPherson Center. Joan helped edit the five journals published by the Museum of Art & History and currently serves on the museum's History Publications Committee. She is a volunteer at Special Collections, University Library, UC Santa Cruz, where she is helping Stanley D. Stevens transcribe and index the Leon Rowland Card Files. It was while indexing the Dorothy Deming Wheeler scrapbooks in 2003 that she met Colleen McInerney-Meagher.

Colleen (left) and Joan. (James M. Morley)

Colleen McInerney-Meagher was born in Hollywood, long before freeways and smog. She fell in love with horses and by the age of eight was playing polo at the Riviera Country Club in Santa Monica. At fourteen she became a member of the Pogonip women's polo team in Santa Cruz, which won the Pacific Coast championship seven years in a row. After raising three children in Los Altos, she retired to Santa Cruz County in 1984. There she became an honorary member of the Pogonip Polo Club, scene of her youthful triumphs. In 1986 to celebrate Pogonip's fiftieth anniversary, she organized and helped mount an exhibit honoring the Pogonip women polo players. Subsequently she helped expand this exhibit for the Octagon Museum of the Santa Cruz County Historical Trust. For more than twenty years, she has been a docent at Elkhorn Slough National Estuarine Research Reserve in Moss Landing. Colleen is currently working on a book about the United States Women's Polo Association, the first and only association dedicated to women's polo.